We hope this book has been informative and helpful on your journey to understanding and celebrating older adults. Thank you for your interest and support!

Title: The Joy of Mindful Tech
Subtitle: Minimalism in the Age of Blockchain and AI

Series: The Joy of Less: A Minimalist's Guide to Happiness
By Lily J. Thompson

"Minimalism is not a lack of something. It's simply the perfect amount of something."
Nicholas Burroughs

"Minimalism is not a style, it is an attitude, a way of being. It's a fundamental reaction against noise, visual noise, disorder, vulgarity. Minimalism is the pursuit of the essence of things, not the appearance."
Claudio Silvestrin

"Minimalism is the intentional promotion of the things we most value and the removal of anything that distracts us from it."
Joshua Becker

"Simplicity is the ultimate sophistication."
Leonardo da Vinci

"The ability to simplify means to eliminate the unnecessary so that the necessary may speak."
Hans Hofmann

"Minimalism is not a lack of personality, it's a matter of emphasizing what's important."
Unknown

"Minimalism is not about living in a stark, empty space. It's about surrounding yourself with the things you love and use most often."
Unknown

Table of Contents

Introduction
What is mindful tech and why is it important

Technology has become an integral part of our lives, from the way we work to the way we communicate and socialize. As technology continues to evolve at a rapid pace, it's important to consider how we can use it mindfully, in a way that benefits both ourselves and the world around us. This is where the concept of "mindful tech" comes in.

What is Mindful Tech?

Mindful tech is the practice of using technology in a way that is intentional, conscious, and aware. It involves being aware of how we use technology and the impact it has on our lives, as well as the environment and society as a whole.

The Importance of Mindful Tech

In today's fast-paced world, it's easy to get caught up in the constant flow of information and the never-ending stream of notifications from our devices. This can lead to stress, anxiety, and a sense of overwhelm. By practicing mindful tech, we can take a step back and approach technology in a way that is more intentional and less reactive.

Beyond its impact on our personal well-being, mindful tech can also have a positive impact on the environment. The production, use, and disposal of technology can have significant environmental consequences, from the mining of raw materials to the energy consumption required to power devices. By using technology mindfully and with intention, we can reduce our environmental impact and contribute to a more sustainable future.

Moreover, technology has the potential to shape our society in significant ways. By using technology mindfully, we can ensure that it is used in a way that promotes equality, fairness, and social justice.

In summary, mindful tech is about using technology in a way that is conscious, intentional, and aware. It's about being aware of how we use technology and the impact it has on ourselves, the environment, and society as a whole. By practicing mindful tech, we can lead more fulfilling and sustainable lives, and contribute to a better world for everyone.

The impact of technology on society and the environment

Technology has had a profound impact on our society and the world around us. From the way we communicate to the way we work and socialize, technology has transformed nearly every aspect of our lives. While technology has brought about many benefits, it has also had significant impacts on both society and the environment.

The Impact of Technology on Society:

Technology has revolutionized the way we live, work, and interact with each other. It has transformed the way we communicate, making it possible to connect with people from around the world instantly. It has also changed the way we work, allowing us to collaborate with others from anywhere and at any time. Moreover, technology has made it possible for us to access a wealth of information with just a few clicks.

However, the impact of technology on society is not all positive. The constant stream of information and notifications from our devices can lead to a sense of overwhelm and addiction. Moreover, technology has transformed the way we interact with each other, leading to a rise in cyberbullying, harassment, and other forms of online abuse. Additionally, technology has disrupted many industries and led to job displacement and inequality.

The Impact of Technology on the Environment:

The production, use, and disposal of technology have significant environmental impacts. The manufacturing process requires the extraction of raw materials, such as metals and minerals, which can have devastating environmental consequences. Moreover, the production process itself requires a significant amount of energy, which contributes to greenhouse gas emissions and climate change.

The use of technology also has environmental impacts. Our devices require energy to operate, and the production of this energy often involves the burning of fossil fuels. Additionally, the disposal of electronic waste is a growing problem, with many devices ending up in landfills or being shipped to developing countries for disposal.

In summary, technology has had a significant impact on both society and the environment. While it has brought about many benefits, it has also had negative consequences that must be addressed. As we continue to use technology in our daily lives, it's important to consider how we can use it in a way that is more mindful and sustainable, both for ourselves and for the world around us. By doing so, we can work towards a future that is both technologically advanced and environmentally responsible.

The role of minimalism in technology

In today's digital age, we are surrounded by technology that promises to make our lives easier and more convenient. However, the constant influx of notifications, messages, and information can also be overwhelming and distracting. In this context, minimalism has emerged as a popular approach to technology, emphasizing simplicity, clarity, and focus. In this section, we will explore the role of minimalism in technology and its potential benefits.

What is Minimalism in Technology?

Minimalism is a design philosophy that emphasizes simplicity, functionality, and the removal of unnecessary elements. In the context of technology, minimalism can be seen in the form of minimalist interfaces, streamlined apps, and digital detox practices. Minimalism in technology aims to help users focus on what matters most, reducing distractions and promoting a sense of calm.

The Role of Minimalism in Technology:

Minimalism has a number of potential benefits when it comes to technology. First and foremost, it can help reduce digital clutter and distraction. By removing unnecessary features, notifications, and interfaces, minimalism can help users stay focused on what they are trying to accomplish.

Additionally, minimalism can help promote mindfulness and intentionality. By being more intentional about the technology we use and how we use it, we can develop a more mindful relationship with our devices. This can help us avoid the mindless scrolling and clicking that can often lead to anxiety, stress, and burnout.

Minimalism can also have environmental benefits. By reducing the number of devices and accessories we use, we can reduce our carbon footprint and the amount of electronic waste we generate. Additionally, minimalist design can help optimize the energy efficiency of our devices.

Finally, minimalism in technology can promote creativity and innovation. By removing unnecessary constraints and focusing on what matters most, minimalist design can help spark new ideas and approaches to technology.

In summary, minimalism has emerged as a popular approach to technology in response to the overwhelming amount of information and distraction we face in today's digital age. By promoting simplicity, focus, and intentionality, minimalism can help us use technology in a more mindful and sustainable way. Furthermore, minimalism can help reduce our carbon footprint, promote creativity and innovation, and ultimately lead to a more fulfilling and balanced relationship with technology.

The benefits of adopting a minimalist approach to tech

In our increasingly digital world, technology has become an essential part of our daily lives. However, with the endless stream of information, notifications, and distractions, it can be easy to get lost in the noise. This is where a minimalist approach to technology comes in. By adopting a minimalist mindset, we can simplify our digital lives, reduce distractions, and achieve a more balanced relationship with technology. In this section, we will explore the benefits of adopting a minimalist approach to tech.

1. Increased Focus:

One of the most significant benefits of adopting a minimalist approach to technology is increased focus. By reducing the number of apps, devices, and notifications that compete for our attention, we can better concentrate on the task at hand. This can lead to increased productivity, better time management, and a more efficient use of our resources.

2. Improved Mental Health:

With the constant barrage of information and notifications, it's easy to become overwhelmed and stressed out. Adopting a minimalist approach to technology can help us reduce these stressors, leading to improved mental health. By intentionally limiting our digital distractions, we can create space for relaxation, self-care, and meaningful interactions with others.

3. Increased Creativity:

A minimalist approach to technology can also spark creativity and innovation. By removing unnecessary constraints and focusing on what matters most, we can discover new ideas and approaches to technology. This can lead to more creative problem-solving, innovative solutions, and a more fulfilling and satisfying relationship with technology.

4. Reduced Environmental Impact:

Another significant benefit of adopting a minimalist approach to technology is a reduced environmental impact. By choosing to use fewer devices and accessories, we can minimize our carbon footprint and reduce the amount of electronic waste we generate. Additionally, minimalist design can help optimize the energy efficiency of our devices.

5. Increased Privacy and Security:

Finally, a minimalist approach to technology can also help us protect our privacy and security online. By reducing our digital footprint and minimizing our exposure to potential threats, we can better safeguard our personal information and online identities.

In summary, adopting a minimalist approach to technology can bring a range of benefits, including increased focus, improved mental health, increased creativity, reduced environmental impact, and increased privacy and security. By intentionally simplifying our digital lives, we can achieve a more balanced and fulfilling relationship with technology. This can lead to a more mindful, sustainable, and fulfilling way of living in the digital age.

Chapter 1: The History of Technology and Minimalism

The evolution of technology and its impact on society

The evolution of technology has had a profound impact on society. Over the centuries, humans have continually developed new technologies to improve their lives, from the invention of the wheel to the development of the internet.

The earliest technologies were simple tools, such as stones and sticks, used for hunting and gathering. These technologies gradually became more advanced, with the development of agriculture leading to the creation of plows and other farming tools. The Industrial Revolution of the 18th and 19th centuries marked a significant turning point in the history of technology, with the development of steam power, machines, and factories transforming the way goods were produced and society was organized.

The 20th century saw the rapid development of electronics, with the invention of the radio, television, and eventually the computer. The internet, which emerged in the 1990s, marked a major turning point in the history of technology, connecting people and information around the world and ushering in the era of digital technology.

The impact of technology on society has been both positive and negative. On the positive side, technology has enabled people to communicate and connect in ways that were once impossible, improving social and economic outcomes. It has also led to significant advances in fields such as medicine, transportation, and energy production, improving the quality of life for people around the world.

However, technology has also had negative impacts on society, particularly in the areas of privacy and inequality. The increasing use of digital technology has raised concerns about data privacy and security, with individuals' personal information vulnerable to theft and misuse. Technology has also contributed to rising income inequality, with some people benefiting greatly from technological advances while others are left behind.

Despite these challenges, the evolution of technology has also given rise to the concept of minimalism, which emphasizes simplicity and efficiency in the use of technology. By focusing on the essential functions of technology and minimizing unnecessary complexity, minimalism can help address some of the negative impacts of technology on society. By using technology in a more mindful and intentional way, people can enjoy its benefits while minimizing its negative impacts on society and the environment.

The emergence of minimalism in tech

As technology continued to evolve and become increasingly integrated into our lives, some people began to question whether this was really a good thing. They noticed that many of the products and services we use on a daily basis are designed to be addictive, keeping us hooked and constantly coming back for more. They also observed that our constant use of technology can have negative effects on our mental health and overall wellbeing.

This dissatisfaction with the state of technology led to the emergence of the minimalist movement in tech. Minimalism is all about simplifying your life by focusing on what's really important and getting rid of anything that doesn't add value. When applied to technology, minimalism means using only the tools and services that are truly necessary and avoiding anything that distracts or detracts from our quality of life.

The minimalist tech movement began to gain traction in the early 2000s, with people experimenting with different ways to simplify their digital lives. This included everything from decluttering their email inboxes and social media accounts to deleting apps and turning off notifications. The goal was to create a more intentional and mindful relationship with technology, one that didn't leave them feeling overwhelmed and stressed out.

Over time, the minimalist tech movement has grown and evolved. Today, there are countless blogs, podcasts, and social media accounts dedicated to the topic, and more and more people are embracing minimalism as a way to improve their relationship with technology. Minimalism in tech has become a way to push back against the forces of constant distraction and information overload, and to reclaim control over our digital lives.

But it's not just individuals who are adopting minimalist tech practices. Some companies are also starting to see the value in creating products and services that are intentionally minimalist. By designing tools and apps that are simple and easy to use, they're able to appeal to a growing segment of consumers who are looking for a more mindful and intentional relationship with technology.

Ultimately, the emergence of minimalism in tech represents a shift in our attitudes towards technology. Rather than blindly accepting the latest gadgets and services that are pushed on us, we're starting to question what truly adds value to our lives and what doesn't. By embracing minimalism, we're able to create a more intentional and mindful relationship with technology, one that supports our wellbeing and helps us to live a more fulfilling life.

The benefits of minimalism in tech historically

Minimalism in technology has a long history dating back to the early days of computing. One of the earliest examples of minimalism in tech is the UNIX operating system, which was developed in the 1960s by a group of programmers at Bell Labs. UNIX was designed to be a minimalist operating system that could run on a variety of hardware platforms. Its minimal design made it highly portable and efficient, and it quickly became popular in academic and research circles.

In the 1980s, Apple Computer introduced the Macintosh, which was a groundbreaking computer that featured a minimalist design. The Macintosh was designed to be easy to use, with a simple graphical user interface that allowed users to perform tasks without needing to know complex commands. This was a stark contrast to other computers of the time, which required users to enter commands in a command-line interface.

One of the biggest benefits of minimalism in tech is that it can lead to increased efficiency and productivity. By eliminating unnecessary features and focusing on the essentials, minimalist tech can be faster and more reliable than more complex systems. This was one of the key advantages of UNIX, which was able to run on a variety of hardware platforms and was highly efficient.

Another benefit of minimalism in tech is that it can lead to a better user experience. By focusing on the essentials and eliminating clutter, minimalist tech can be easier to use and more intuitive. This was one of the key advantages of the Macintosh, which was able to make computing accessible to a wider audience by simplifying the user interface.

Minimalism in tech has also played an important role in the development of the internet. The early days of the internet were characterized by simple, text-based interfaces that were easy to use and navigate. This minimal design was key to the success of early internet services like email and bulletin board systems, which were able to reach a wide audience due to their simplicity and ease of use.

Finally, minimalism in tech has played an important role in the development of mobile devices. The first smartphones were characterized by minimalist designs that focused on the essentials. This approach has continued to be important in the development of modern smartphones, which are designed to be simple and intuitive to use.

Overall, the history of technology has been marked by many examples of minimalism in tech, which have led to increased efficiency, better user experiences, and the development of new technologies. By focusing on the essentials and eliminating clutter, minimalist tech has played an important role in shaping the way we use technology today.

The drawbacks and criticisms of minimalism in tech

Minimalism in technology has its benefits, but it also has its drawbacks and criticisms. Some of these drawbacks and criticisms include:

1. Limited Functionality: One of the main criticisms of minimalism in technology is that it limits the functionality of devices and software. In order to achieve minimalism, features and functions are often removed or simplified, which can make devices less useful for certain tasks.

2. Lack of Innovation: Some critics argue that minimalism in technology can stifle innovation. By focusing on simplicity and functionality, minimalism may discourage developers from exploring new and creative ideas.

3. Limited Appeal: Minimalist designs may not appeal to everyone, and some users may prefer devices or software with more features and customization options.

4. Difficulty in Implementation: Implementing minimalism in technology can be challenging, as it requires careful consideration of which features are essential and which can be removed or simplified. This process can be time-consuming and may require significant changes to the design and development process.

5. Incompatibility: Minimalist designs may not be compatible with certain types of users or use cases. For

example, minimalist software may not be suitable for professional use or for users with specific accessibility needs.

Despite these criticisms, minimalism in technology remains a popular and effective approach for many users and developers. By focusing on simplicity and functionality, minimalism can help reduce clutter, increase efficiency, and improve the user experience. It is important, however, to consider the potential drawbacks and limitations of minimalism and to carefully evaluate whether it is the right approach for a particular project or device.

Chapter 2: The Basics of Blockchain
Understanding the fundamentals of blockchain technology

Blockchain is a distributed ledger technology that allows for secure, transparent, and tamper-proof record-keeping. At its core, it is a decentralized database that maintains a continuously growing list of records, called blocks, which are linked and secured using cryptography.

To understand blockchain technology, it's helpful to think of it as a digital ledger that keeps track of all transactions in a network. The ledger is maintained by a network of nodes, which are computers that are connected to the network. Each node has a copy of the ledger, and when a new transaction occurs, it is broadcast to all nodes in the network.

When a node receives a new transaction, it verifies its authenticity and then adds it to a block. Each block contains a set of transactions, along with a unique digital signature, called a hash, that identifies the block and links it to the previous block in the chain. This creates an unbreakable chain of blocks, hence the name "blockchain."

One of the key features of blockchain technology is its decentralization. There is no central authority that controls the blockchain, and all transactions are processed by the network of nodes. This means that there is no need for intermediaries, such as banks or other financial institutions, to verify and process transactions. This can lead to faster and cheaper transactions, as well as increased security and transparency.

Another important aspect of blockchain technology is its security. Because each block is linked to the previous block using cryptography, it is virtually impossible to tamper with the records in the blockchain. This makes blockchain technology ideal for applications where security and trust are paramount, such as financial transactions, supply chain management, and voting systems.

In summary, blockchain technology is a distributed ledger technology that allows for secure, transparent, and tamper-proof record-keeping. Its key features include decentralization, security, and transparency, which make it well-suited for a variety of applications.

The benefits and limitations of blockchain

Blockchain technology is being hailed as one of the most important technological innovations of our time. It has the potential to revolutionize the way we do business, govern, and interact with each other online. But like any technology, it comes with its own set of benefits and limitations.

Let's start with the benefits. One of the biggest advantages of blockchain is that it is a decentralized system. This means that there is no central authority that controls the flow of data or transactions. Instead, all participants in the network have a copy of the same ledger and work together to validate transactions. This creates a level of transparency and accountability that is hard to achieve with traditional centralized systems.

Another benefit of blockchain is its security. The technology uses cryptographic algorithms to ensure that data is kept secure and cannot be tampered with. This makes it virtually impossible for hackers to attack the system and steal data or funds. Additionally, because all participants in the network have a copy of the same ledger, it becomes very difficult to manipulate or corrupt data.

Blockchain technology is also incredibly efficient. Transactions can be processed much faster and at a lower cost than traditional methods, such as wire transfers or credit card transactions. This is because there are no intermediaries involved in the process, which reduces transaction fees and processing times.

However, blockchain technology also has its limitations. One of the biggest challenges facing blockchain is scalability. Currently, most blockchain networks can only handle a limited number of transactions per second. This makes it difficult to use the technology for high-volume applications, such as global payment systems.

Another limitation of blockchain is its complexity. The technology is still in its early stages, and many people find it difficult to understand. This can make it challenging for businesses and governments to adopt and implement the technology.

Finally, there are concerns about the environmental impact of blockchain. The process of verifying transactions on a blockchain network requires a lot of computational power, which can be very energy-intensive. As more and more people start using blockchain technology, there are concerns about the carbon footprint of the technology.

Overall, blockchain technology has a lot of potential to transform the way we do business and interact with each other online. But like any technology, it comes with its own set of benefits and limitations. It is up to us to carefully consider these factors and decide how best to use blockchain to create a more efficient, secure, and transparent world.

The relationship between minimalism and blockchain

In recent years, minimalism has become a popular concept in the world of blockchain technology. Minimalism in this context refers to the idea of designing blockchain systems that are simple, efficient, and effective in meeting their intended purpose.

One of the primary benefits of minimalism in blockchain is improved scalability. Blockchain systems that are designed with a minimalist approach can handle large volumes of transactions while maintaining high speeds and low costs. By minimizing the complexity of the system, blockchain developers can reduce the processing time required to validate transactions, resulting in faster processing times.

Another benefit of minimalism in blockchain is increased security. By simplifying the blockchain system, developers can eliminate unnecessary features that can introduce vulnerabilities. A minimalist blockchain system reduces the attack surface and makes it more difficult for attackers to exploit any weaknesses.

Furthermore, minimalism in blockchain has the potential to increase decentralization. By minimizing the number of nodes required to validate transactions, a blockchain system can become more accessible to a wider range of users. This can help to prevent the centralization of power that can occur when a small number of nodes control the majority of the network.

Despite these benefits, there are also some limitations to minimalism in blockchain. For example, a minimalist approach may not be suitable for all types of blockchain applications. Some applications may require more complex features that cannot be achieved through a minimalist design. Additionally, minimalism may not always be the most efficient approach, as some features may need to be added to meet the specific needs of a particular application.

Despite these limitations, the relationship between minimalism and blockchain is an important one. By adopting a minimalist approach to blockchain development, developers can create systems that are more efficient, secure, and accessible. As blockchain technology continues to evolve, it is likely that we will see more emphasis on minimalism and its role in shaping the future of this important technology.

Real-world applications of blockchain technology

Blockchain technology has gained a lot of attention in recent years due to its potential to transform various industries. Here are some real-world applications of blockchain technology:

1. Cryptocurrencies: Cryptocurrencies are digital currencies that use blockchain technology to enable secure, decentralized transactions. Bitcoin, the first and most popular cryptocurrency, is built on blockchain technology. Other cryptocurrencies, such as Ethereum and Litecoin, also use blockchain technology.

2. Supply chain management: Blockchain technology can be used to track products from their origin to the final destination, providing an immutable record of every transaction along the way. This can be used to ensure the authenticity and quality of products, as well as to reduce the risk of fraud and counterfeiting.

3. Voting systems: Blockchain technology can be used to create secure, transparent, and tamper-proof voting systems. By using blockchain technology, it is possible to create a voting system that is immune to fraud, hacking, and other forms of tampering.

4. Healthcare: Blockchain technology can be used to securely store and share medical records, enabling patients

to have complete control over their medical data. This can be particularly useful in emergency situations where quick access to medical records can be critical.

5. Banking and finance: Blockchain technology can be used to create a more secure and transparent financial system. By using blockchain technology, it is possible to create a system where transactions are recorded and verified in a decentralized and transparent way, reducing the risk of fraud and increasing trust in the financial system.

6. Identity verification: Blockchain technology can be used to create secure and tamper-proof digital identities. By using blockchain technology, it is possible to create a system where individuals have complete control over their digital identity, reducing the risk of identity theft and fraud.

7. Real estate: Blockchain technology can be used to create a more transparent and efficient real estate market. By using blockchain technology, it is possible to create a system where real estate transactions are recorded and verified in a decentralized and transparent way, reducing the risk of fraud and increasing trust in the real estate market.

These are just a few examples of the real-world applications of blockchain technology. As the technology continues to evolve, it is likely that we will see more and more innovative uses of blockchain technology in various industries.

Chapter 3: The Basics of AI
Understanding the fundamentals of AI technology

Artificial intelligence, or AI, is a rapidly advancing field of computer science that involves developing machines that can perform tasks that typically require human intelligence. At its core, AI is about creating algorithms and systems that can analyze data, recognize patterns, and make decisions based on that information.

One of the key features of AI is its ability to learn and improve over time. This is done through the use of machine learning algorithms, which enable the system to adapt and improve its performance based on feedback from the data it processes.

AI technology is typically divided into two main categories: narrow or weak AI, and general or strong AI. Narrow AI is designed to perform specific tasks, such as playing chess or recognizing images. General AI, on the other hand, is intended to be more versatile and adaptable, with the ability to learn and reason across a wide range of tasks and contexts.

There are many different applications for AI technology, ranging from voice assistants like Siri and Alexa to self-driving cars and advanced medical diagnostic tools. As the field continues to advance, it is likely that we will see

AI systems playing an increasingly important role in many areas of our lives. However, there are also concerns about the potential risks and drawbacks of this technology, such as the risk of job displacement and the ethical considerations around the use of AI in decision-making processes.

Overall, AI is a complex and rapidly evolving field with many exciting possibilities and challenges. As with any technology, it is important to approach it with caution and to carefully consider its potential benefits and risks.

The benefits and limitations of AI

Artificial Intelligence (AI) is a field of computer science that aims to create intelligent machines that can perform tasks that would typically require human intelligence, such as visual perception, speech recognition, decision-making, and natural language processing. AI has become increasingly prevalent in various industries, including healthcare, finance, transportation, and entertainment. The benefits of AI are numerous and diverse, but it also poses several limitations and challenges.

One of the main benefits of AI is its ability to automate routine tasks and streamline operations, thereby saving time and reducing costs. For instance, chatbots powered by AI technology can be used in customer service to answer common queries and resolve issues, freeing up human agents to focus on more complex tasks. AI can also be used in healthcare to analyze medical records and identify potential health risks, allowing doctors to provide personalized treatment plans for their patients.

AI technology also has the potential to improve safety and security, for instance, by detecting and preventing cyber attacks and fraud. AI-powered autonomous vehicles can also reduce human error in driving and decrease the number of road accidents. Additionally, AI technology can enhance scientific research by analyzing large datasets and identifying patterns that humans may not be able to detect.

However, AI also has some limitations and challenges that need to be addressed. One of the main limitations of AI is its reliance on large datasets, which can be biased and incomplete. This can result in the AI system making inaccurate predictions or decisions. There is also a risk of AI technology being used for malicious purposes, such as cyber attacks or data breaches. Furthermore, the increasing automation of tasks through AI may lead to job displacement and social inequality.

To address these limitations and challenges, researchers and policymakers need to work together to ensure that AI technology is developed and used ethically and responsibly. This includes ensuring that AI systems are transparent and accountable, and that they are designed to mitigate the risk of bias and errors. Additionally, policymakers should consider the potential impact of AI on employment and work towards creating new job opportunities that are not susceptible to automation.

In summary, AI technology has numerous benefits and applications, but it also poses several challenges and limitations. By addressing these challenges and ensuring that AI is developed and used responsibly, we can maximize the benefits of this technology while minimizing its potential risks.

The relationship between minimalism and AI

Artificial intelligence (AI) and minimalism may seem like two unrelated concepts, but they are actually closely connected in many ways. In this chapter, we will explore the relationship between minimalism and AI.

To start, let's define minimalism. Minimalism is a lifestyle philosophy that emphasizes living with less, simplifying one's life, and removing excess. It's about focusing on what's essential and removing distractions that don't add value to one's life.

When it comes to AI, minimalism can be applied in a few different ways. One way is through the development of minimalist AI algorithms. These algorithms are designed to be simple and efficient, with the goal of achieving high performance with minimal computational resources. By keeping the algorithms simple, they can be easier to understand, debug, and maintain. Minimalist AI algorithms can be particularly useful in resource-constrained environments, such as mobile devices, where power and computational resources are limited.

Another way that minimalism and AI are related is through the application of minimalist design principles to AI systems. Minimalist design emphasizes simplicity, clarity, and functionality. By applying minimalist design principles to AI systems, designers can create interfaces that are intuitive and easy to use. This is particularly important in applications such as virtual assistants or chatbots, where users expect a seamless and intuitive experience.

Minimalism can also be applied to the ethical considerations surrounding AI. As AI becomes increasingly powerful and ubiquitous, there is a growing concern about the potential negative impacts it could have on society. One way to mitigate these risks is through a minimalist approach to AI development. This means focusing on developing AI systems that are designed to be transparent, trustworthy, and aligned with human values. By keeping the goals of AI development simple and focused on human needs, we can help ensure that AI is developed in a way that benefits society as a whole.

However, there are also potential drawbacks to a minimalist approach to AI. One concern is that minimalist AI algorithms may not be as accurate or powerful as more complex ones. In some cases, a more complex algorithm may be necessary to achieve the desired level of performance. Additionally, there is a risk that a minimalist approach could lead to oversimplification of complex problems, which could result in unintended consequences.

In conclusion, while there are both benefits and drawbacks to a minimalist approach to AI, the two concepts are closely related. By applying minimalist principles to AI development, we can create systems that are efficient, intuitive, and aligned with human values. However, it's important to recognize that there may be cases where a more complex approach is necessary to achieve the desired level of performance. Ultimately, the goal should be to develop AI systems that are both powerful and responsible, with a focus on benefiting society as a whole.

Real-world applications of AI technology

Artificial intelligence (AI) is one of the most rapidly growing fields of technology today, with applications in almost every industry imaginable. In this chapter, we will explore the real-world applications of AI, including some of the most innovative and impactful uses of this technology.

1. Healthcare: AI has the potential to revolutionize healthcare, with applications such as personalized medicine, drug discovery, and medical image analysis. Personalized medicine involves using AI algorithms to analyze a patient's genetic makeup and medical history to create personalized treatment plans. Drug discovery involves using AI to analyze vast amounts of data and identify potential new drug candidates. Medical image analysis uses AI algorithms to analyze medical images, such as X-rays and MRIs, to help doctors diagnose and treat patients.

2. Financial services: AI is being used in the financial industry to automate processes such as fraud detection, risk assessment, and trading. For example, AI algorithms can analyze large amounts of data to identify patterns and anomalies that could indicate fraudulent activity. AI is also being used in trading to analyze market data and make predictions about future market trends.

3. Transportation: Self-driving cars are perhaps the most well-known application of AI in transportation. However, AI is also being used to optimize traffic flow, reduce congestion, and improve public transportation. For example, AI algorithms can analyze real-time traffic data to identify the most efficient routes for public transportation.

4. Retail: AI is being used in the retail industry to improve the customer experience and increase sales. For example, AI algorithms can analyze customer data to create personalized recommendations and offers. AI-powered chatbots are also being used to provide customer service and support.

5. Manufacturing: AI is being used in manufacturing to optimize processes and increase efficiency. For example, AI algorithms can analyze sensor data to identify potential equipment failures before they occur. AI is also being used to optimize supply chains and reduce waste.

6. Education: AI is being used in education to personalize learning and improve student outcomes. For example, AI-powered tutoring systems can analyze student data to identify areas where a student needs additional support and provide personalized recommendations. AI is also being used to analyze student data to identify factors that contribute to academic success.

7. Entertainment: AI is being used in the entertainment industry to create personalized experiences for consumers. For example, streaming services are using AI algorithms to analyze user data and make recommendations for content based on their viewing history.

Overall, AI has the potential to transform almost every industry and aspect of our lives. While there are certainly limitations and challenges to be addressed, the potential benefits of AI make it an exciting and rapidly evolving field to watch.

Chapter 4: The Minimalist Approach to Tech
The principles of minimalist tech

The minimalist approach to tech is centered around the idea of simplifying and decluttering one's digital life. By reducing the number of devices, apps, and digital distractions, individuals can focus on what truly matters and enhance their overall well-being.

Here are some of the principles of minimalist tech:

1. Intentionality: The first principle of minimalist tech is being intentional about what you choose to keep in your digital life. This means taking the time to evaluate whether each app, device, or service is essential and adds value to your life. By intentionally selecting the digital tools you use, you can avoid the unnecessary clutter that can overwhelm and distract you.

2. Simplicity: A minimalist approach to tech values simplicity and ease of use. This means choosing digital tools that are straightforward and uncomplicated, with minimal features and distractions. Simple tech allows you to focus on what's important and reduces the cognitive load that comes with using complex systems.

3. Quality over quantity: In minimalist tech, quality is valued over quantity. Instead of having multiple devices that serve similar purposes, or using a plethora of apps that do

the same thing, minimalist tech focuses on high-quality tools that serve a specific purpose well.

4. Mindfulness: Being mindful of how you use technology is an important principle of minimalist tech. This means paying attention to how much time you spend on your devices, and being present in the moment rather than getting lost in digital distractions. By using technology with intention and awareness, you can cultivate a healthier relationship with digital tools and avoid the negative consequences of excessive use.

5. Sustainability: A minimalist approach to tech also values sustainability. This means choosing devices and services that are environmentally friendly and have a minimal impact on the planet. By reducing your digital footprint, you can contribute to a more sustainable future.

Overall, the principles of minimalist tech aim to help individuals use technology in a way that enhances their lives and well-being, rather than detracting from it. By intentionally selecting high-quality digital tools that are simple and sustainable, individuals can create a more mindful and fulfilling relationship with technology.

Strategies for implementing minimalism in tech

Now that we understand the principles of minimalist tech, the question arises: how can we implement minimalism in our daily use of technology? Below are some strategies for incorporating minimalist principles into our tech habits.

1. Evaluate your current tech usage: The first step towards minimalism is to evaluate your current tech usage. Take stock of the devices you use, the apps you have installed, and the websites you visit. Identify the ones you use the most and the ones you can do without.

2. Eliminate the unnecessary: Once you've identified the apps, devices, and websites you use the least, it's time to eliminate them. Uninstall apps you rarely use and unsubscribe from newsletters and notifications that you don't find useful.

3. Simplify your devices: Consider simplifying your tech devices by opting for ones that serve multiple purposes. For example, instead of having a separate device for music, a separate device for email, and a separate device for web browsing, opt for a tablet or laptop that can handle all of these tasks.

4. Prioritize privacy: Minimalism in tech also means prioritizing your privacy. Review the privacy policies of the

apps and websites you use and opt for ones that collect less data or offer more control over your data.

5. Embrace analog alternatives: Sometimes, the best way to implement minimalism in tech is to embrace analog alternatives. For example, instead of using a digital to-do list app, consider using a physical notebook. Instead of listening to music on a streaming service, consider buying vinyl records.

6. Set boundaries: Finally, set boundaries for yourself when it comes to tech usage. Create designated tech-free zones in your home, such as the bedroom or dining table. Set aside specific times of the day for checking email and social media, and avoid checking them outside of those times.

By incorporating these strategies into your tech habits, you can adopt a more minimalist approach to technology and reap the benefits that come with it. Not only will you experience less stress and distraction, but you'll also have more time and mental space for the things that matter most in your life.

The benefits of a minimalist tech approach

As we have discussed earlier, adopting a minimalist approach to technology can bring numerous benefits to our lives. In this section, we will delve deeper into these benefits and how they can make a significant impact on our daily routines.

1. Increased Productivity: Minimalism in tech can help us stay focused on our tasks and minimize distractions. By limiting the number of apps, notifications, and gadgets, we can free up mental space and achieve more in less time.

2. Improved Mental Health: Excessive use of technology can have adverse effects on our mental health, such as anxiety, stress, and depression. By reducing our screen time and creating boundaries around our tech usage, we can improve our overall well-being and have more time for self-care.

3. Enhanced Creativity: Minimalism in tech can help us tap into our creative potential. By eliminating distractions and spending more time in solitude, we can give our minds the freedom to explore new ideas and generate innovative solutions.

4. Better Relationships: Spending too much time on our screens can negatively impact our relationships with friends and family. By reducing our dependence on

technology, we can focus on building meaningful connections and improving our communication skills.

5. Reduced Environmental Impact: The production and disposal of technology have a significant environmental impact. By embracing a minimalist approach to tech, we can reduce our carbon footprint and contribute to a more sustainable future.

6. Financial Benefits: Technology can be expensive, and a minimalist approach can help us save money by focusing on essential gadgets and services. By avoiding unnecessary upgrades and subscriptions, we can reduce our expenses and increase our financial stability.

Overall, adopting a minimalist approach to technology can have a positive impact on various aspects of our lives. By prioritizing what truly matters and focusing on what adds value, we can lead more intentional and fulfilling lives.

Minimalism in technology has gained popularity among individuals and companies alike. Many are realizing the benefits of minimizing tech usage and finding ways to incorporate it into their daily lives and work. In this chapter, we will explore examples of companies and individuals who practice minimalist tech.

1. Apple Apple is one of the most well-known companies that have adopted minimalist principles in their products. From their hardware design to software features, they strive for simplicity and ease of use. The minimalist design of their products has garnered them a massive following, and their products are highly sought after.

2. Google Google is another company that has embraced minimalist principles in their products. They have streamlined their search engine to provide users with the most relevant information quickly. They have also created a minimalist interface for their email service, Gmail, which has made it incredibly popular among users.

3. Tesla Tesla is a car company that has gained massive popularity for their electric vehicles. Their cars are known for their sleek, minimalist design and innovative features. Tesla's CEO, Elon Musk, is also known for his

minimalist approach to life and work, which has contributed to the company's success.

4. Marie Kondo Marie Kondo is a Japanese organizing consultant and author who has gained a massive following for her minimalist approach to decluttering and organizing. Her method, known as the KonMari method, involves keeping only the items that spark joy in a person's life and getting rid of the rest. Her approach has inspired people to simplify their lives and reduce clutter.

5. Tim Ferriss Tim Ferriss is an American author, entrepreneur, and podcaster who has embraced minimalism in his work and personal life. He is known for his book, "The 4-Hour Work Week," which encourages people to focus on the most important tasks and eliminate unnecessary work. He also advocates for simplifying personal possessions and reducing clutter to increase productivity and reduce stress.

6. Leo Babauta Leo Babauta is a blogger and author who has gained a massive following for his blog, "Zen Habits." He advocates for a minimalist lifestyle and provides practical tips for simplifying various aspects of life, including work, relationships, and personal possessions. His approach has inspired many people to live a more intentional and fulfilling life.

7. Joshua Fields Millburn and Ryan Nicodemus Joshua Fields Millburn and Ryan Nicodemus are the founders of the Minimalists, a popular blog, podcast, and documentary series that promotes a minimalist lifestyle. They encourage people to question their possessions and focus on the things that truly matter in life. Their approach has resonated with many people who are seeking a simpler and more intentional life.

In conclusion, minimalist tech principles have been adopted by many individuals and companies who are seeking a simpler, more intentional way of living and working. These examples show that minimalist tech can be applied to various aspects of life and work, and can lead to increased productivity, reduced stress, and greater fulfillment.

Chapter 5: Mindful Consumption in the Digital Age
The impact of digital consumption on the environment

In today's digital age, we are constantly consuming information, entertainment, and products through our digital devices such as smartphones, laptops, and tablets. However, the convenience of digital consumption comes with an environmental cost. This chapter will explore the impact of digital consumption on the environment and the steps we can take to reduce our digital carbon footprint.

Energy Consumption One of the biggest impacts of digital consumption on the environment is the energy consumption required to power the devices we use. Data centers that store and process our digital information consume a significant amount of energy. According to a 2019 report by the International Energy Agency (IEA), data centers accounted for 1% of global electricity consumption and 0.3% of global CO_2 emissions, a figure that is expected to triple by 2030.

In addition to data centers, the energy required to manufacture and transport digital devices also contributes to their environmental impact. According to a report by the European Environmental Bureau (EEB), the manufacturing of a single smartphone requires approximately 14 kg of CO_2

emissions, which is equivalent to the amount of CO2 produced by driving a car for 100 km.

E-waste Another environmental impact of digital consumption is e-waste. E-waste refers to the disposal of electronic devices, which can contain hazardous materials such as lead, mercury, and cadmium. According to a 2019 report by the United Nations, the world produced 53.6 million metric tons of e-waste, and only 17.4% of it was recycled. The rest ended up in landfills or was illegally traded, causing harm to the environment and human health.

Internet Overload The constant consumption of digital content also contributes to internet overload. The more people consume and share digital content, the more strain it puts on the internet infrastructure. This can lead to slower internet speeds, and the need to build more data centers to keep up with the demand.

Reducing Your Digital Carbon Footprint While digital consumption may seem unavoidable, there are steps we can take to reduce our digital carbon footprint. One way is to use digital devices and services more mindfully. This means being aware of the energy consumption required for the devices and services we use and minimizing our usage accordingly. For example, turning off devices when not in use, using energy-efficient settings, and reducing screen time.

Another way to reduce our digital carbon footprint is to choose more sustainable devices and services. This includes selecting devices with a longer lifespan, buying second-hand devices, and choosing services that use renewable energy sources.

Finally, recycling electronic devices properly can help reduce e-waste. Many countries and organizations have e-waste recycling programs in place that can help ensure that electronic devices are disposed of safely and sustainably.

Conclusion The impact of digital consumption on the environment is significant, and it's up to each of us to take responsibility for our digital carbon footprint. By using digital devices and services more mindfully, choosing more sustainable options, and properly recycling electronic devices, we can reduce our environmental impact and work towards a more sustainable digital future.

The benefits of mindful consumption in tech

The digital age has brought with it countless benefits and conveniences, but it has also given rise to new problems, such as the negative impact of digital consumption on our well-being and the environment. However, there is a growing movement towards mindful consumption in tech, which focuses on being intentional about our use of technology in order to reduce our impact and improve our lives. In this section, we will explore the benefits of mindful consumption in tech.

1. Reduced Environmental Impact

One of the most significant benefits of mindful consumption in tech is a reduced environmental impact. The production, use, and disposal of electronic devices contribute to environmental problems such as pollution, resource depletion, and greenhouse gas emissions. By being mindful of our tech consumption, we can reduce our overall impact on the environment.

For example, we can:

- Choose to repair or refurbish our devices instead of buying new ones

- Opt for energy-efficient devices and power-saving settings

- Use digital products and services that prioritize sustainability and ethical practices

- Recycle or dispose of electronic devices properly, rather than contributing to e-waste

2. Improved Well-being

Another benefit of mindful consumption in tech is improved well-being. The constant use of technology can have negative effects on our mental health, such as increased stress, anxiety, and addiction. By being more intentional about our tech use, we can reduce these negative effects and improve our overall well-being.

For example, we can:

- Set boundaries and limits on our tech use, such as designated screen-free times and places

- Use mindfulness techniques to reduce stress and increase self-awareness

- Choose digital products and services that prioritize user privacy and well-being

- Prioritize face-to-face communication and social interaction over digital communication

3. Increased Productivity and Focus

Mindful consumption in tech can also lead to increased productivity and focus. The constant distraction and interruptions of technology can make it difficult to concentrate and get things done. By being intentional about our tech use, we can reduce distractions and increase our ability to focus on important tasks.

For example, we can:

- Turn off notifications and limit our use of social media and other distracting apps

- Use productivity tools and apps that help us stay organized and focused

- Take breaks and prioritize self-care to avoid burnout and exhaustion

- Choose digital products and services that prioritize simplicity and functionality over excess features and distractions

In conclusion, mindful consumption in tech has many benefits, including a reduced environmental impact, improved well-being, and increased productivity and focus. By being intentional about our use of technology and prioritizing our values, we can create a healthier and more sustainable relationship with technology.

Strategies for reducing digital consumption

In today's fast-paced digital world, it's easy to get lost in the endless sea of notifications, emails, and social media feeds. Many people find themselves spending hours mindlessly scrolling through their screens, often at the expense of their mental health, productivity, and overall well-being. The good news is that there are several strategies that you can adopt to reduce your digital consumption and reclaim your time and energy. Here are some effective ways to get started:

1. Set Boundaries

The first step to reducing digital consumption is to set boundaries. This means being intentional about the time and space you allocate to technology. One way to do this is to establish a tech-free zone in your home or workplace, such as your bedroom or dining area. Another way is to set specific times of the day when you will check your email, social media, or other apps. For example, you could check your email only twice a day, once in the morning and once in the afternoon, and avoid checking it outside those designated times.

2. Turn Off Notifications

Notifications can be a major distraction and can interrupt your work, conversations, or leisure time. To reduce digital consumption, consider turning off notifications for non-essential apps or turning off your phone altogether during certain times of the day. This way, you can focus on the task at hand without being constantly bombarded by alerts and updates.

3. Practice Mindful Consumption

Mindful consumption means being intentional about what you consume online and how much time you spend doing it. This involves being aware of your browsing habits and consciously choosing to engage with content that is meaningful and relevant to your goals and interests. To practice mindful consumption, ask yourself before clicking on a link or scrolling through a feed, "Is this adding value to my life? Is this something I truly need to see or read?"

4. Digital Detox

Sometimes, the best way to reduce digital consumption is to take a break from technology altogether. A digital detox involves unplugging from all devices and screens for a designated period, such as a day, weekend, or week. During this time, you can focus on other activities that bring you joy and fulfillment, such as spending time in nature, reading a book, or spending quality time with friends and family.

5. Use Technology to Your Advantage

While reducing digital consumption is important, it's also important to remember that technology can be a useful tool when used intentionally. To make technology work for you, consider using productivity apps that help you stay organized and focused, or meditation apps that help you manage stress and improve your mental health. By using technology in a mindful way, you can enhance your productivity, creativity, and overall well-being.

6. Develop a Support System

Reducing digital consumption can be challenging, especially if you're used to being constantly connected. To make the process easier, consider developing a support system, such as a group of friends or family members who are also committed to reducing their digital consumption. You can hold each other accountable, share tips and strategies, and provide encouragement and motivation.

In conclusion, reducing digital consumption is an important aspect of mindful consumption in the digital age. By setting boundaries, turning off notifications, practicing mindful consumption, taking a digital detox, using technology to your advantage, and developing a support system, you can reduce your digital consumption and enhance your overall well-being.

The relationship between mindful consumption and minimalism in tech

In recent years, the concepts of minimalism and mindful consumption have gained traction as people become more aware of the impact of their daily choices on the environment and their own well-being. These two concepts intersect in the realm of technology, where individuals are seeking ways to reduce their digital consumption while still enjoying the benefits of technology.

Minimalism in tech emphasizes simplicity and functionality, and this approach can also be applied to mindful consumption. When we become more mindful of our technology usage, we can identify what is truly essential and eliminate the excess that clutters our digital lives. This, in turn, reduces our overall digital consumption.

Here are some ways in which mindful consumption and minimalism in tech are related:

1. Prioritizing what matters: Both minimalism in tech and mindful consumption involve prioritizing what truly matters to us. By focusing on what is important and necessary, we can reduce our consumption of digital content and technology.

2. Simplifying our technology usage: Minimalism in tech encourages us to simplify our digital lives by eliminating

unnecessary apps, devices, and subscriptions. This approach also helps us to reduce our digital consumption by streamlining our technology usage.

3. Encouraging intentional technology use: Mindful consumption emphasizes the importance of intentional choices, and this can be applied to technology usage as well. By being more intentional with how we use technology, we can reduce our overall consumption while still benefiting from its many advantages.

4. Reducing distractions: Digital distractions can be a major source of wasted time and energy. Both minimalism in tech and mindful consumption encourage us to eliminate distractions and focus on what truly matters.

5. Promoting well-being: Mindful consumption and minimalism in tech both promote well-being by encouraging us to be more intentional with our choices. By reducing our digital consumption and focusing on what truly matters, we can improve our overall well-being and quality of life.

In essence, mindful consumption and minimalism in tech are two sides of the same coin. By combining these two approaches, we can reduce our digital consumption while still benefiting from the many advantages that technology offers. Ultimately, this approach allows us to live more intentionally and mindfully, leading to a more fulfilling and sustainable lifestyle.

Chapter 6: The Ethics of Technology
The ethical considerations of technology

Technology has become an integral part of our lives, and with its increasing role comes the need to consider the ethical implications of its use. There are a variety of ethical considerations that arise in the context of technology, from privacy and security concerns to the impact of technology on society and the environment. In this chapter, we will explore some of the key ethical considerations of technology and what they mean for individuals and society as a whole.

Privacy and Security One of the most significant ethical considerations of technology is privacy and security. As we share more and more of our personal information online, the risk of that information being compromised or misused also increases. For example, social media platforms and search engines collect vast amounts of data about their users, which can be used to target advertising or even manipulate individuals' beliefs and behaviors. Additionally, data breaches and cyberattacks can result in the theft of sensitive information, such as financial or healthcare data.

As technology continues to evolve, the need for strong privacy and security protections becomes more pressing. Individuals must be able to trust that their data is being handled responsibly and that they have control over how it is used. Companies and organizations also have a responsibility to protect their users' data and to be transparent about how that data is being used.

Impact on Society Another ethical consideration of technology is its impact on society. While technology has the potential to bring significant benefits, such as increased efficiency and access to information, it can also have negative consequences. For example, automation and artificial intelligence have the potential to eliminate jobs, leading to economic inequality and social unrest. Social media platforms can also contribute to the spread of misinformation and polarization, creating a more divided society.

It is important to consider the potential impact of technology on society as a whole, rather than simply focusing on individual benefits or drawbacks. This requires careful thought and consideration, as well as a willingness to make changes when necessary to ensure that technology is being used in a responsible and beneficial way.

Environmental Impact The environmental impact of technology is also an important ethical consideration. The production and disposal of electronic devices contribute to environmental problems such as pollution, resource depletion, and climate change. Additionally, the energy consumption of data centers and other technology infrastructure can be significant, contributing to greenhouse gas emissions and other environmental problems.

As technology continues to become more ubiquitous, it is important to consider its environmental impact and to take steps to mitigate its effects. This can include measures such as designing devices with longer lifespans, using more sustainable materials in production, and using renewable energy to power data centers.

Bias and Discrimination Finally, the potential for bias and discrimination in technology is another important ethical consideration. For example, algorithms used in hiring or loan decisions may be biased against certain groups, leading to unequal outcomes. Similarly, facial recognition technology has been shown to be less accurate when used on individuals with darker skin tones, leading to concerns about its potential use in law enforcement.

It is important to ensure that technology is designed and implemented in a way that is fair and unbiased. This may require addressing underlying social and economic inequalities, as well as carefully considering the potential impact of technology on marginalized groups.

Conclusion The ethical considerations of technology are complex and multifaceted, requiring careful thought and consideration. By being mindful of the potential impact of technology on privacy, society, the environment, and equality, individuals and organizations can work to ensure that technology is being used in a responsible and beneficial way. Ultimately, the ethical use of technology is essential for creating a more just and equitable society.

The role of minimalism in ethical tech

As we continue to develop and use technology in our daily lives, it's important to consider the ethical implications of these advancements. From data privacy concerns to the impact of technology on job displacement, ethical considerations are an integral part of the technology conversation.

One approach to promoting ethical technology is through the lens of minimalism. By embracing a minimalist approach, we can prioritize ethical considerations in the development and use of technology. Here are some ways in which minimalism can play a role in promoting ethical tech:

1. Simplifying technology: By embracing a minimalist approach, we can simplify technology and avoid unnecessary complexity. This can help reduce the potential for ethical issues such as data breaches or unintended consequences of technology use.

2. Promoting transparency: Minimalism encourages transparency in the development and use of technology. This means that companies should be upfront about their data collection practices and the intended use of data collected. This can help users make informed decisions about how their data is used and promote trust between users and tech companies.

3. Prioritizing user experience: A minimalist approach to technology puts the user first. This means creating technology that is intuitive, easy to use, and designed with the user in mind. This can help promote ethical use of technology by making it more accessible and less intimidating for users.

4. Reducing waste: Minimalism encourages us to reduce waste in all aspects of our lives, including technology. This means considering the environmental impact of technology and striving to create products and services that are sustainable and environmentally responsible.

5. Encouraging ethical behavior: Finally, a minimalist approach to technology can encourage ethical behavior by promoting values such as simplicity, honesty, and transparency. This can create a culture of ethical tech use and help hold tech companies accountable for their actions.

While minimalism is not a silver bullet solution to all ethical considerations in technology, it can be a valuable tool in promoting ethical behavior and responsible use of technology. By prioritizing simplicity, transparency, and the user experience, we can create technology that is both useful and ethical.

Technology has transformed the way we live our lives, and as our reliance on technology increases, so do the ethical considerations that come with it. From privacy concerns to automation of jobs, there are numerous examples of ethical dilemmas that arise from the use of technology. In this section, we will explore some of the most notable ethical dilemmas in tech.

1. Data Privacy: One of the biggest ethical concerns with technology is data privacy. Tech companies collect vast amounts of data from users, including personal information, online behavior, and location data. This data is often used for targeted advertising or sold to third-party companies. The Cambridge Analytica scandal, in which millions of Facebook users had their data harvested without their consent, highlights the importance of protecting user data.

2. Algorithmic Bias: Machine learning algorithms are becoming increasingly popular in decision-making processes, from hiring to loan approvals. However, these algorithms can be biased, perpetuating discrimination against certain groups. For example, Amazon had to scrap its AI recruiting tool after it was found to be biased against women.

3. Automation of Jobs: The automation of jobs is another ethical dilemma in tech. As machines become more capable, there is a risk that many jobs will become obsolete, leaving people without work and without a source of income. This raises questions about the responsibility of tech companies to help workers transition to new industries.

4. Artificial Intelligence: As AI technology advances, it raises ethical questions about its use. For example, the use of autonomous weapons, such as drones, raises concerns about the ability to make ethical decisions in the absence of human intervention. There are also concerns about the use of AI for surveillance, which could be used to violate privacy rights.

5. Social Media: Social media platforms have given individuals a powerful voice, but they have also been used to spread hate speech and misinformation. Social media companies are grappling with how to balance free speech with the need to protect users from harmful content.

6. Cybersecurity: With the increasing amount of personal information being stored online, cybersecurity has become a major ethical concern. Companies have a responsibility to protect user data from hackers and cybercriminals, but they also have a responsibility to disclose data breaches to users in a timely and transparent manner.

7. Digital Divide: The digital divide refers to the gap between those who have access to technology and those who do not. As technology becomes more pervasive, there is a risk that those without access to technology will be left behind, exacerbating existing inequalities. Tech companies have a responsibility to address the digital divide by providing access to technology to marginalized communities.

In conclusion, technology has brought about many benefits, but it has also raised numerous ethical concerns. It is important for individuals and companies to consider the ethical implications of their use of technology and to work towards finding solutions to these challenges. By doing so, we can ensure that technology is used in a responsible and ethical way that benefits society as a whole.

Strategies for ethical tech practices

As technology continues to rapidly advance and become more integrated into our daily lives, it is important to consider the ethical implications of these developments. Ethical tech practices can help ensure that technology is used in a responsible and beneficial way that prioritizes the well-being of individuals and society as a whole. Here are some strategies for ethical tech practices:

1. Prioritize User Privacy: One of the most important ethical considerations in tech is the protection of user privacy. This can include implementing strong data security measures, being transparent about data collection and usage, and allowing users to control their own data. Companies and individuals should always consider the potential risks and benefits of collecting and sharing user data, and ensure that users are informed and consenting to the use of their data.

2. Foster Inclusivity and Diversity: Technology should be accessible and usable for all people, regardless of their background or abilities. Ethical tech practices should prioritize inclusivity and diversity, such as designing products and services that are user-friendly and accessible for people with disabilities or from different cultural backgrounds. Companies and individuals should also strive

to eliminate bias and discrimination in the design and implementation of technology.

3. Ensure Transparency and Accountability: It is important for companies and individuals to be transparent about their use of technology, including how it is designed, developed, and used. Ethical tech practices should prioritize transparency and accountability, including being open about potential risks and benefits, and engaging in ongoing dialogue with stakeholders to ensure that technology is being used in a responsible and beneficial way.

4. Consider the Social and Environmental Impact: The use of technology can have significant social and environmental impacts, and ethical tech practices should consider these impacts when designing and using technology. This can include considering the environmental footprint of technology, such as its energy consumption and waste generation, as well as the potential social impacts, such as the displacement of jobs or the amplification of inequalities.

5. Empower Users: Users should have control over the technology they use and be empowered to make informed decisions about how they engage with technology. Ethical tech practices should prioritize user empowerment, including providing users with information about their data

and privacy, and allowing them to customize their experience and control their own data.

6. Embrace Minimalism: The minimalist approach to tech can also be a valuable strategy for ethical tech practices. By prioritizing simplicity and functionality, minimalist tech can reduce the potential for harmful or unethical uses of technology, and prioritize the well-being of users over profit or other incentives.

7. Engage in Ongoing Learning and Reflection: Technology is constantly evolving, and ethical tech practices should prioritize ongoing learning and reflection. This can include staying up-to-date on the latest developments in technology and their ethical implications, as well as engaging in ongoing reflection about the potential risks and benefits of technology use.

Overall, ethical tech practices should prioritize the well-being of individuals and society as a whole, and consider the potential social, environmental, and ethical impacts of technology use. By implementing these strategies, we can ensure that technology is used in a responsible and beneficial way that supports our collective well-being.

Chapter 7: The Future of Minimalist Tech

Emerging trends in minimalist tech

As technology continues to evolve, minimalist tech has emerged as a counter-movement to the overwhelming complexity and overconsumption of the digital age. Here are some emerging trends in minimalist tech that are shaping the future of technology:

1. Simplicity and Minimalism: As more people embrace minimalism and simplicity in their daily lives, technology is following suit. This trend is evidenced in the popularity of minimalist interfaces and design. Companies are shifting towards user-friendly and intuitive interfaces, which create a more streamlined and effortless user experience.

2. Sustainable Tech: Environmental consciousness is becoming increasingly important in the tech industry. Many companies are investing in green energy, recyclable materials, and other sustainable practices to reduce their carbon footprint. Consumers are also becoming more aware of the impact of their digital consumption on the environment and are seeking out sustainable tech alternatives.

3. Digital Detox and Mindful Tech Use: The rise of digital addiction has prompted a movement towards mindful

tech use and digital detoxing. Consumers are looking for ways to disconnect from technology and develop healthy relationships with their devices. Companies are developing tools and resources to help users manage their tech usage and cultivate more mindful habits.

4. Privacy and Security: As the amount of personal data being collected and shared online continues to grow, privacy and security are becoming more important concerns. Consumers are demanding greater control over their personal information and are seeking out tech products and services that prioritize privacy and security.

5. Ethical Tech: With the increasing influence of technology in our lives, ethical considerations are becoming more important. Companies are being held accountable for the impact of their products and services on society, and consumers are demanding more ethical tech solutions. This includes everything from transparency in data collection to responsible AI development.

6. Augmented Reality: Augmented reality (AR) is an emerging technology that integrates digital elements into the real world. AR has the potential to create immersive and interactive experiences that can enhance productivity, education, and entertainment. Minimalist tech is exploring

how AR can be used to enhance simplicity and minimalism in various fields.

7. Artificial Intelligence: Artificial intelligence (AI) has the potential to revolutionize how we interact with technology. Minimalist tech is exploring how AI can be used to create more efficient and intuitive interfaces and streamline complex tasks. However, ethical concerns surrounding AI development and usage must also be considered.

In conclusion, minimalist tech is not just a passing trend but a movement towards simplicity, sustainability, mindfulness, and ethics in technology. As technology continues to evolve, these emerging trends will shape the future of technology and guide us towards a more mindful and responsible digital age.

The impact of minimalist tech on society and the environment

The rise of minimalist tech has the potential to bring about significant positive impacts on both society and the environment. As people become more mindful of their technology consumption habits and shift towards minimalism, they can reduce the negative effects of excessive technology use and promote sustainability.

One of the most significant ways that minimalist tech can impact society is by improving well-being. By adopting minimalist tech practices, people can reduce the amount of time they spend on technology and instead focus on other activities that promote physical, mental, and emotional health. For example, people might spend more time engaging in physical activity, spending time with loved ones, or pursuing hobbies that bring them joy. By prioritizing these activities, people can improve their overall quality of life and reduce the negative effects of technology addiction, such as anxiety, depression, and social isolation.

In addition to improving well-being, minimalist tech can also help promote sustainability and reduce the negative environmental impacts of technology. One of the primary ways this is accomplished is through the reduction of e-waste. As people shift towards minimalism, they tend to consume fewer electronics and dispose of them less frequently. This can help reduce the amount of electronic waste that ends up in landfills, where it can take hundreds of years to decompose and release harmful toxins into the environment.

Another way that minimalist tech can promote sustainability is through energy conservation. Many electronics consume significant amounts of energy, and the production and distribution of that energy can have significant negative environmental impacts. By consuming fewer electronics and adopting energy-saving practices, people can reduce their overall energy consumption and promote sustainability.

Finally, minimalist tech can also promote social and environmental justice. Many of the materials and resources required to produce electronics are sourced from developing countries, where labor and environmental regulations may be lax or nonexistent. This can result in the exploitation of workers and significant environmental degradation. By reducing demand for electronics and promoting sustainable practices, people can help reduce these negative impacts and promote more just and equitable systems of production and consumption.

In conclusion, minimalist tech has the potential to bring about significant positive impacts on both society and the environment. By reducing excessive technology consumption, people can improve well-being, promote sustainability, and support more just and equitable systems of production and consumption. As the trend towards minimalist tech continues to grow, we can expect to see more significant positive impacts on society and the environment in the years to come.

The potential benefits and drawbacks of minimalist tech

As technology continues to advance, the minimalist approach to tech is becoming increasingly popular. While this approach offers numerous benefits, it also presents certain drawbacks. In this section, we'll explore both the potential benefits and drawbacks of minimalist tech.

Potential Benefits of Minimalist Tech:

1. Increased Productivity: One of the biggest benefits of minimalist tech is increased productivity. By minimizing distractions, simplifying tasks, and prioritizing focus, people can get more done in less time. This approach can lead to a greater sense of accomplishment, satisfaction, and even happiness.

2. Reduced Stress: Another benefit of minimalist tech is that it can help reduce stress levels. By minimizing the number of apps, emails, and notifications that compete for our attention, people can create a calmer, more peaceful environment. This can lead to lower stress levels, improved mental health, and better overall well-being.

3. Improved Health: By reducing the amount of time spent using tech devices, minimalist tech can also lead to improved physical health. Research has shown that prolonged use of technology can lead to poor posture, eye

strain, and other physical health problems. By practicing mindful consumption and minimalism in tech, people can reduce their risk of these health issues.

4. Environmental Benefits: By using technology less and adopting a minimalist approach to tech, individuals can also contribute to environmental sustainability. Fewer devices and less consumption can lead to less e-waste, which is a major contributor to environmental pollution.

5. Financial Savings: Adopting a minimalist tech approach can also lead to financial savings. By buying fewer devices and using them for longer, individuals can save money on the cost of purchasing new devices, as well as on energy costs associated with their use.

Potential Drawbacks of Minimalist Tech:

1. Limited Functionality: One of the main drawbacks of minimalist tech is that it may not offer the same functionality as more advanced devices. For example, a minimalist phone may not have all the features and capabilities of a smartphone. This limitation can be challenging for people who rely on certain features and apps for their work or personal life.

2. Social Isolation: Another potential drawback of minimalist tech is that it can lead to social isolation. By using technology less and reducing digital consumption, people

may miss out on important social interactions and opportunities. Additionally, minimalism can lead to a lack of diversity in the media and information people consume, which can be detrimental to personal growth and understanding.

3. Learning Curve: Adopting a minimalist approach to tech can also require a significant learning curve. People may need to adjust to new devices or platforms, which can be challenging and time-consuming.

4. Compatibility Issues: Another potential issue with minimalist tech is that it may not be compatible with certain software or hardware. This can be particularly problematic for people who rely on specific tools or programs for their work.

5. Job Disruption: Finally, minimalist tech can also potentially disrupt certain industries and job markets. For example, the rise of automation and AI may lead to job loss in certain sectors, while the decline of traditional media may lead to fewer job opportunities in journalism and other related fields.

Conclusion:

As we can see, the minimalist approach to tech has both potential benefits and drawbacks. By prioritizing productivity, reducing stress, improving health, and contributing to environmental sustainability, minimalist tech can offer many advantages. However, it can also lead to limited functionality, social isolation, a steep learning curve, compatibility issues, and potential job disruption. As technology continues to evolve, it's important to carefully consider the impact of minimalist tech and make informed decisions about its adoption.

Predictions for the future of minimalist tech

The minimalist approach to technology has gained momentum in recent years, and many experts predict that it will continue to grow in popularity. Here are some predictions for the future of minimalist tech:

1. Increased Focus on Sustainability: With climate change becoming a more pressing issue, there will be a greater emphasis on sustainability in technology. Minimalist tech will play a significant role in reducing e-waste and encouraging more responsible consumption of electronics.

2. Growth of Minimalist Product Lines: As more consumers embrace minimalist tech, there will likely be an increase in the number of minimalist product lines. Companies may develop simpler, more streamlined devices that are designed with minimalism in mind, as well as products that are specifically marketed to the minimalist community.

3. Continued Rise of the Digital Minimalism Movement: The digital minimalism movement is already gaining traction, and it is likely to continue to grow in popularity. More people are becoming aware of the negative effects of digital overload and are seeking ways to reduce their dependence on technology.

4. Increasing Emphasis on Privacy: As technology continues to become more integrated into our daily lives, privacy concerns will become more prevalent. Minimalist tech may offer a solution to these concerns by providing simpler, more transparent products that are designed to protect user privacy.

5. Greater Demand for Tech-Free Spaces: As people become more aware of the negative effects of technology on mental health, there will likely be a greater demand for tech-free spaces. These spaces may be dedicated to mindfulness, relaxation, or simply unplugging from technology for a period of time.

6. New Technologies that Support Minimalism: As minimalist tech continues to gain popularity, there will likely be new technologies that emerge to support this movement. For example, we may see new software and apps that help people reduce their digital clutter or make it easier to use technology in a more mindful way.

7. Increased Collaboration between Minimalist and Sustainable Tech Movements: The minimalist and sustainable tech movements share many of the same goals, and we may see more collaboration between these two communities in the future. Together, they can work to create a more responsible and sustainable approach to technology.

Overall, the future of minimalist tech looks bright. As more people become aware of the benefits of a simpler, more mindful approach to technology, we can expect to see a continued shift toward minimalist tech products and practices. By prioritizing sustainability, privacy, and mindfulness, we can create a more responsible and balanced relationship with technology.

Chapter 8: Minimalism in Action: Case Studies
Case studies of companies and individuals who practice minimalist tech

In this chapter, we will examine case studies of companies and individuals who have successfully implemented minimalist tech practices into their daily routines. By studying these examples, we can gain insights into how minimalist tech can be applied in various contexts, and how it can lead to more productive and fulfilling lives.

1. Apple

Apple is known for its sleek and minimalist design aesthetic, and this approach extends to its technology as well. Apple's products are designed to be user-friendly and intuitive, with a focus on simplicity and functionality. The company has also implemented a number of eco-friendly practices, such as using recycled materials in its products and minimizing packaging waste.

2. Google

Google has a reputation for being a leader in innovative technology, but the company also places a high value on minimalist design. Its products, such as the Google search engine and the Chrome browser, are designed to be easy to use and visually appealing. Google has also implemented a number of initiatives to reduce its environmental impact, such as using renewable energy sources and reducing water usage.

3. Marie Kondo

Marie Kondo is a Japanese organizing consultant and author who has gained worldwide fame for her minimalist approach to home organization. Her philosophy, known as the KonMari method, encourages people to declutter their homes and keep only the possessions that bring them joy. Kondo's methods have been adapted by many people and have inspired a broader movement towards minimalism in various aspects of life.

4. Leo Babauta

Leo Babauta is the creator of Zen Habits, a popular blog focused on mindfulness and minimalism. Babauta's writing emphasizes the importance of simplifying one's life and reducing distractions in order to achieve greater focus and clarity. He also emphasizes the importance of sustainability and reducing one's environmental impact.

5. Joshua Fields Millburn and Ryan Nicodemus

Joshua Fields Millburn and Ryan Nicodemus are the creators of The Minimalists, a blog and podcast focused on minimalist living. The duo promotes the idea that living with less can lead to greater happiness and fulfillment, and they offer practical tips for simplifying one's life. They also place a strong emphasis on the environmental benefits of minimalist living.

6. Colin Wright

Colin Wright is a writer and minimalist who has gained a large following through his blog, books, and speaking engagements. Wright's philosophy emphasizes the importance of intentional living and the pursuit of experiences over possessions. He has also written extensively on the environmental benefits of minimalism and sustainable living.

7. Tiny Houses

The tiny house movement is a growing trend in minimalist living that involves living in smaller, more efficient homes. These homes are often designed to be eco-friendly, with features such as solar panels, composting toilets, and rainwater collection systems. The movement has gained popularity in recent years as a way to reduce environmental impact and simplify one's life.

In conclusion, these case studies demonstrate the diverse ways in which minimalist tech can be applied in various contexts. From tech giants like Apple and Google to individual bloggers and lifestyle experts, minimalist tech has proven to be a powerful tool for achieving greater focus, clarity, and sustainability. By studying these examples, we can gain valuable insights into how to incorporate minimalist tech practices into our own lives, and how to work towards a more mindful and fulfilling future.

The benefits and challenges of minimalist tech in action

Minimalist tech is gaining momentum as a way to reduce stress, increase productivity, and decrease the environmental impact of technology. As we've seen in previous chapters, minimalist tech is about being intentional with our use of technology and focusing on what truly matters.

In this chapter, we will explore case studies of companies and individuals who practice minimalist tech and the benefits and challenges they have encountered.

Benefits of Minimalist Tech in Action

1. Increased Productivity: Companies that have adopted minimalist tech practices have seen an increase in productivity. By eliminating distractions and focusing on essential tasks, employees can complete work efficiently.

2. Reduced Stress: Individuals who practice minimalist tech report feeling less overwhelmed and stressed. By reducing screen time and notifications, they can focus on other activities and live in the present moment.

3. Enhanced Creativity: Minimalist tech can also promote creativity. By stepping away from screens and technology, individuals can stimulate their minds and generate new ideas.

4. Improved Mental Health: Mindful use of technology can have a positive impact on mental health. By reducing exposure to negative content, individuals can avoid feelings of anxiety and depression.

Challenges of Minimalist Tech in Action

1. Resistance to Change: Adopting minimalist tech practices can be challenging for individuals and companies who are used to traditional tech practices. It requires a shift in mindset and habits, which can be difficult.

2. Fear of Missing Out (FOMO): Individuals may fear missing out on important information or social events if they limit their use of technology. This fear can make it challenging to adopt minimalist tech practices.

3. Increased Responsibility: Minimalist tech practices require individuals to take more responsibility for their use of technology. Without relying on notifications and constant connectivity, individuals must be more proactive in managing their time and tasks.

4. Limited Access: In some cases, minimalist tech practices may limit access to certain resources or information. For example, reducing screen time may limit access to news and information sources.

Case Studies of Minimalist Tech in Action

1. Basecamp: Basecamp is a software company that creates collaboration tools for remote teams. They have a strict no-meeting policy and prioritize asynchronous communication to reduce distractions and interruptions.

2. Digital Minimalism by Cal Newport: Cal Newport is a computer science professor and author of "Digital Minimalism," which advocates for mindful use of technology. He practices minimalist tech by limiting his use of social media and using a flip phone instead of a smartphone.

3. A Life Less Throwaway by Tara Button: Tara Button is the founder of BuyMeOnce, a company that promotes sustainable consumerism. She practices minimalist tech by limiting her use of technology and promoting products that are durable and long-lasting.

4. The Slow Home Podcast: The Slow Home Podcast is a podcast that promotes intentional living and minimalism. Hosts Brooke McAlary and Ben McAlary encourage listeners to reduce their dependence on technology and focus on what truly matters.

Conclusion

The benefits of minimalist tech in action are clear: increased productivity, reduced stress, enhanced creativity, and improved mental health. However, challenges such as resistance to change and fear of missing out must be overcome to fully realize these benefits.

Case studies of companies and individuals who practice minimalist tech provide real-world examples of how these practices can be implemented successfully. By taking responsibility for our use of technology and being intentional with our choices, we can achieve a more mindful and fulfilling relationship with technology.

Lessons learned from successful minimalist tech implementations

Minimalism is not just a philosophy; it is a way of life that can be applied to everything, including technology. As the world becomes more technologically advanced, it's important to consider how we can use it in a more minimalist way. In this chapter, we will look at some successful case studies of minimalist tech implementations and the lessons we can learn from them.

Case Study 1: Apple

Apple is a company that is known for its minimalist design. From its sleek and simple hardware designs to its clean and easy-to-use software interfaces, Apple has always placed a high value on minimalism. Apple's minimalist approach has resulted in a loyal customer base that appreciates the company's focus on simplicity and ease of use.

One of the key lessons we can learn from Apple is the importance of focusing on the user experience. By keeping things simple and easy to use, Apple has created products that appeal to a broad range of users, regardless of their level of technical expertise. This is an important lesson for any company or individual looking to implement minimalist tech.

Case Study 2: Google

Google is another company that has embraced minimalism in its design and user interfaces. The company's search engine, for example, is a model of minimalist design, with a clean and uncluttered interface that focuses solely on delivering relevant search results.

Google's minimalist approach has also been applied to its hardware products, such as the Chromebook, which is a simple and affordable laptop that is designed for basic computing needs. The Chromebook is a great example of how minimalist tech can be used to create affordable and accessible products for a broad range of users.

One of the key lessons we can learn from Google is the importance of simplicity in design. By keeping things simple and focusing on the essentials, Google has created products that are easy to use and accessible to a wide range of users.

Case Study 3: Leo Babauta

Leo Babauta is a blogger and author who has embraced minimalist tech in his personal and professional life. Babauta is the founder of the popular blog Zen Habits, which focuses on simplicity, minimalism, and mindfulness. He is also the author of several books on minimalism and productivity.

Babauta's approach to minimalist tech is centered around the idea of simplifying his digital life. This includes using simple tools and software, minimizing distractions, and focusing on the essentials. Babauta has found that by simplifying his tech, he is able to be more productive and focused on the things that matter most to him.

One of the key lessons we can learn from Babauta is the importance of being intentional about our use of technology. By being mindful of how we use technology, we can make better choices about which tools and platforms we use, and how we use them. This can help us to be more productive, less stressed, and more fulfilled in our daily lives.

Conclusion

These case studies provide valuable insights into the benefits of minimalist tech and the lessons we can learn from successful implementations. Whether you are an individual looking to simplify your digital life or a company looking to create minimalist tech products, these case studies demonstrate that simplicity and focus are key to success.

By focusing on the user experience, simplicity in design, and being intentional about our use of technology, we can create minimalist tech products and practices that are accessible, affordable, and easy to use. As technology continues to evolve, it is important that we embrace minimalism as a way to create products and practices that are both ethical and sustainable.

The potential for scale and impact with minimalist tech

The rise of minimalist tech has shown us that less is often more when it comes to technology. In this chapter, we explore the potential for scale and impact with minimalist tech, particularly when it comes to creating solutions for the world's most pressing problems.

Minimalist tech can help address a range of issues, from environmental sustainability to social justice to healthcare. By focusing on simplicity, efficiency, and user-centered design, minimalist tech can create solutions that are more accessible, affordable, and effective than traditional technology.

One example of the potential for minimalist tech to create impact is in the field of healthcare. Traditional medical devices and equipment can be expensive, complex, and difficult to use, particularly in low-resource settings. Minimalist tech solutions, such as low-cost diagnostic tools and mobile health apps, can help address these challenges and improve access to healthcare for underserved populations.

Another area where minimalist tech can have a significant impact is in environmental sustainability. The world is facing urgent environmental challenges, from climate change to resource depletion to pollution. Minimalist tech solutions, such as energy-efficient devices, sustainable materials, and circular economy models, can help address these challenges and create a more sustainable future.

In addition to healthcare and environmental sustainability, minimalist tech can also play a role in social justice. Technology has the power to connect people, amplify voices, and facilitate social change. Minimalist tech solutions, such as community-driven platforms, digital storytelling tools, and open-source software, can help empower communities and facilitate social movements.

However, while the potential for impact with minimalist tech is significant, there are also challenges to overcome. One challenge is the need to balance simplicity with functionality. Minimalist tech solutions should be simple and easy to use, but they also need to be effective and meet the needs of their users. Achieving this balance requires a deep understanding of user needs and a commitment to user-centered design.

Another challenge is the need to scale and sustain minimalist tech solutions. Creating effective solutions is just the first step; to create real impact, these solutions need to be scaled and adopted widely. This requires strong partnerships, funding, and support, as well as a commitment to ongoing evaluation and improvement.

Despite these challenges, the potential for scale and impact with minimalist tech is significant. By focusing on simplicity, efficiency, and user-centered design, minimalist tech solutions can create meaningful change in a range of fields. The key is to remain committed to these principles and to work collaboratively to create solutions that are accessible, affordable, and effective for all.

Conclusion

The potential for technology and minimalism to create a more sustainable and fulfilling future

The world we live in today is constantly evolving, and technology is at the forefront of that evolution. With advancements in technology, we have been able to accomplish things we never thought possible. However, with great power comes great responsibility. The negative impact of technology on the environment and our lives has become more apparent, and it is clear that something must be done.

Minimalism is a movement that has gained traction in recent years, as people seek to simplify their lives and reduce their impact on the environment. The principles of minimalism can be applied to technology, and this has led to the emergence of minimalist tech. This new approach to technology is focused on creating products and services that are simple, efficient, and sustainable.

In this book, we have explored the benefits and challenges of minimalist tech, as well as strategies for reducing digital consumption and ethical considerations in technology. We have also looked at case studies of companies and individuals who have successfully implemented minimalist tech, and the lessons we can learn from them.

As we conclude this book, it is clear that the potential for technology and minimalism to create a more sustainable and fulfilling future is immense. By adopting minimalist tech, we can reduce our impact on the environment, increase our productivity, and live more fulfilling lives. We can also ensure that technology is used in a responsible and ethical way, with the interests of society and the environment at its core.

The potential for scale and impact with minimalist tech is enormous. With the right approach and mindset, we can transform the way we interact with technology and create a better future for ourselves and future generations. We must work together to create a more sustainable and fulfilling future, and minimalist tech can help us achieve this goal.

In conclusion, this book has been an exploration of the possibilities and potential of minimalist tech. We hope that it has inspired you to think differently about technology and its role in your life, and that you will join us on this journey towards a more sustainable and fulfilling future.

The challenges and opportunities of adopting a minimalist tech approach

As we wrap up our exploration of minimalist tech, it's important to consider both the challenges and opportunities that come with adopting this approach. While minimalist tech has the potential to create a more sustainable and fulfilling future, there are also significant obstacles to overcome.

One of the main challenges of minimalist tech is the entrenched cultural norms and economic incentives that drive the technology industry. As we've seen throughout this book, the prevailing business model for tech companies is to maximize user engagement and monetize data. This means that many of the devices, apps, and platforms we use are designed to be addictive and time-consuming, rather than efficient and purposeful.

To shift towards minimalist tech, we'll need to find ways to incentivize companies to prioritize sustainability, ethical practices, and user well-being. This may require regulatory changes, as well as changes in consumer behavior. For example, if we start valuing products that are durable, repairable, and designed to last, rather than disposable and replaceable, companies will have more of an incentive to invest in sustainable practices.

Another challenge of minimalist tech is that it requires a certain level of privilege and access. Not everyone has the luxury of being able to disconnect from technology or choose to use more expensive, but sustainable products. In order to create a truly equitable and sustainable future, we'll need to address issues of economic inequality and ensure that everyone has access to the resources they need to make informed choices about their tech use.

Despite these challenges, there are many opportunities that come with adopting a minimalist tech approach. For one, minimalist tech can help us live more intentionally and deliberately. By reducing our digital distractions and focusing on the tools and devices that truly serve our needs, we can create more space for the things that matter most, whether that's building meaningful relationships, pursuing creative hobbies, or simply enjoying the present moment.

Minimalist tech can also help us reduce our carbon footprint and mitigate the negative impacts of technology on the environment. By choosing products that are designed to last, we can reduce the amount of waste we produce and conserve resources. By being more intentional about our tech use, we can also reduce our energy consumption and carbon emissions.

Finally, adopting a minimalist tech approach can help us foster more ethical and sustainable values in our society. As we've seen throughout this book, technology has the power to shape our beliefs, behaviors, and norms in powerful ways. By consciously choosing to use technology in ways that align with our values, we can help create a more just and sustainable future for everyone.

In conclusion, minimalist tech is not a one-size-fits-all solution, and there are certainly challenges to overcome. However, by being intentional and deliberate about our tech use, we can create a more sustainable and fulfilling future for ourselves and our communities. Whether we're individual consumers, tech companies, or policymakers, we all have a role to play in shaping the future of technology in ways that serve the greater good.

The call to action for individuals and organizations to embrace mindful tech practices

As we conclude our exploration of minimalist tech, it is clear that there is a pressing need for individuals and organizations to embrace mindful tech practices. We have seen the potential benefits of minimalism, including increased productivity, reduced environmental impact, and improved well-being. However, there are also significant challenges to implementing a minimalist tech approach, including the need for behavior change, the pressure to keep up with technological advancements, and the difficulty of balancing sustainability with profitability.

Despite these challenges, the potential rewards of adopting a minimalist tech approach are too great to ignore. The growing concern about the environmental impact of technology, the negative effects on mental health, and the need for more sustainable business practices all point towards the necessity of embracing mindful tech practices.

For individuals, adopting a minimalist tech approach means being more intentional about our technology use. We can start by examining our own habits and identifying areas where we can reduce our digital consumption. We can also prioritize ethical tech practices, such as choosing products from companies that prioritize sustainability and privacy, and advocating for policies that protect consumer rights.

For organizations, embracing minimalist tech practices can lead to improved productivity and sustainability, while also enhancing brand reputation and customer loyalty. Companies can start by implementing policies that prioritize sustainable tech practices, such as reducing e-waste and promoting energy-efficient technologies. Additionally, companies can adopt ethical tech practices that prioritize user privacy and data protection.

In conclusion, the call to action for individuals and organizations is clear. It is time to embrace mindful tech practices and take steps towards a more sustainable and fulfilling future. By working together to prioritize ethical and sustainable tech practices, we can create a world where technology serves us, rather than the other way around. It is up to all of us to make a difference and shape the future of technology in a positive way.

Introduction

What is mindful tech and why is it important

Technology has become an integral part of our lives, from the way we work to the way we communicate and socialize. As technology continues to evolve at a rapid pace, it's important to consider how we can use it mindfully, in a way that benefits both ourselves and the world around us. This is where the concept of "mindful tech" comes in.

What is Mindful Tech?

Mindful tech is the practice of using technology in a way that is intentional, conscious, and aware. It involves being aware of how we use technology and the impact it has on our lives, as well as the environment and society as a whole.

The Importance of Mindful Tech

In today's fast-paced world, it's easy to get caught up in the constant flow of information and the never-ending stream of notifications from our devices. This can lead to stress, anxiety, and a sense of overwhelm. By practicing mindful tech, we can take a step back and approach technology in a way that is more intentional and less reactive.

Beyond its impact on our personal well-being, mindful tech can also have a positive impact on the environment. The production, use, and disposal of technology can have significant environmental consequences, from the mining of raw materials to the energy consumption required to power devices. By using technology mindfully and with intention, we can reduce our environmental impact and contribute to a more sustainable future.

Moreover, technology has the potential to shape our society in significant ways. By using technology mindfully, we can ensure that it is used in a way that promotes equality, fairness, and social justice.

In summary, mindful tech is about using technology in a way that is conscious, intentional, and aware. It's about being aware of how we use technology and the impact it has on ourselves, the environment, and society as a whole. By practicing mindful tech, we can lead more fulfilling and sustainable lives, and contribute to a better world for everyone.

The impact of technology on society and the environment
Technology has had a profound impact on our society and the world around us. From the way we communicate to the way we work and socialize, technology has transformed nearly every aspect of our lives. While technology has brought about many benefits, it has also had significant impacts on both society and the environment.

The Impact of Technology on Society:
Technology has revolutionized the way we live, work, and interact with each other. It has transformed the way we

communicate, making it possible to connect with people from around the world instantly. It has also changed the way we work, allowing us to collaborate with others from anywhere and at any time. Moreover, technology has made it possible for us to access a wealth of information with just a few clicks.

However, the impact of technology on society is not all positive. The constant stream of information and notifications from our devices can lead to a sense of overwhelm and addiction. Moreover, technology has transformed the way we interact with each other, leading to a rise in cyberbullying, harassment, and other forms of online abuse. Additionally, technology has disrupted many industries and led to job displacement and inequality.

The Impact of Technology on the Environment:

The production, use, and disposal of technology have significant environmental impacts. The manufacturing process requires the extraction of raw materials, such as metals and minerals, which can have devastating environmental consequences. Moreover, the production process itself requires a significant amount of energy, which contributes to greenhouse gas emissions and climate change. The use of technology also has environmental impacts. Our devices require energy to operate, and the production of this energy often involves the burning of fossil fuels. Additionally, the disposal of electronic waste is a growing problem, with many devices ending up in landfills or being shipped to developing countries for disposal.

In summary, technology has had a significant impact on both society and the environment. While it has brought about many benefits, it has also had negative consequences that must be addressed. As we continue to use technology in our daily lives, it's important to consider how we can use it in a way that is more mindful and sustainable, both for ourselves and for the world around us. By doing so, we can work towards a future that is both technologically advanced and environmentally responsible.

The role of minimalism in technology

In today's digital age, we are surrounded by technology that promises to make our lives easier and more convenient. However, the constant influx of notifications, messages, and information can also be overwhelming and distracting. In this context, minimalism has emerged as a popular approach to technology, emphasizing simplicity, clarity, and focus. In this section, we will explore the role of minimalism in technology and its potential benefits.

What is Minimalism in Technology?

Minimalism is a design philosophy that emphasizes simplicity, functionality, and the removal of unnecessary elements. In the context of technology, minimalism can be seen in the form of minimalist interfaces, streamlined apps, and digital detox practices. Minimalism in technology aims to help users focus on what matters most, reducing distractions and promoting a sense of calm.

The Role of Minimalism in Technology:

Minimalism has a number of potential benefits when it comes to technology. First and foremost, it can help reduce digital clutter and distraction. By removing unnecessary features, notifications, and interfaces, minimalism can help users stay focused on what they are trying to accomplish.

Additionally, minimalism can help promote mindfulness and intentionality. By being more intentional about the technology we use and how we use it, we can develop a more mindful relationship with our devices. This can help us avoid the mindless scrolling and clicking that can often lead to anxiety, stress, and burnout.

Minimalism can also have environmental benefits. By reducing the number of devices and accessories we use, we can reduce our carbon footprint and the amount of electronic waste we generate. Additionally, minimalist design can help optimize the energy efficiency of our devices.

Finally, minimalism in technology can promote creativity and innovation. By removing unnecessary constraints and focusing on what matters most, minimalist design can help spark new ideas and approaches to technology.

In summary, minimalism has emerged as a popular approach to technology in response to the overwhelming amount of information and distraction we face in today's digital age. By promoting simplicity, focus, and intentionality, minimalism can help us use technology in a more mindful and sustainable way. Furthermore, minimalism can help reduce our carbon footprint, promote creativity and innovation, and ultimately lead to a more fulfilling and balanced relationship with technology.

The benefits of adopting a minimalist approach to tech
In our increasingly digital world, technology has become an essential part of our daily lives. However, with the endless stream of information, notifications, and distractions, it can be easy to get lost in the noise. This is where a minimalist approach to technology comes in. By adopting a minimalist mindset, we can simplify our digital lives, reduce distractions, and achieve a more balanced relationship with technology. In this section, we will explore the benefits of adopting a minimalist approach to tech.

1. Increased Focus:

One of the most significant benefits of adopting a minimalist approach to technology is increased focus. By reducing the number of apps, devices, and notifications that compete for our attention, we can better concentrate on the task at hand. This can lead to increased productivity, better time management, and a more efficient use of our resources.

2. Improved Mental Health:

With the constant barrage of information and notifications, it's easy to become overwhelmed and stressed out. Adopting a minimalist approach to technology can help us reduce these stressors, leading to improved mental health. By intentionally limiting our digital distractions, we can create space for relaxation, self-care, and meaningful interactions with others.

3. Increased Creativity:

A minimalist approach to technology can also spark creativity and innovation. By removing unnecessary constraints and focusing on what matters most, we can discover new ideas and approaches to technology. This can lead to more creative problem-solving, innovative solutions, and a more fulfilling and satisfying relationship with technology.

4. Reduced Environmental Impact:

Another significant benefit of adopting a minimalist approach to technology is a reduced environmental impact. By choosing to use fewer devices and accessories, we can minimize our carbon footprint and reduce the amount of electronic waste we generate. Additionally, minimalist design can help optimize the energy efficiency of our devices.

5. Increased Privacy and Security:

Finally, a minimalist approach to technology can also help us protect our privacy and security online. By reducing our digital footprint and minimizing our exposure to potential threats, we can better safeguard our personal information and online identities.

In summary, adopting a minimalist approach to technology can bring a range of benefits, including increased focus, improved mental health, increased creativity, reduced environmental impact, and increased privacy and security. By intentionally simplifying our digital lives, we can achieve a more balanced and fulfilling relationship with technology. This can lead to a more mindful, sustainable, and fulfilling way of living in the digital age.

Chapter 1: The History of Technology and Minimalism
The evolution of technology and its impact on society

The evolution of technology has had a profound impact on society. Over the centuries, humans have continually developed new technologies to improve their lives, from the invention of the wheel to the development of the internet.

The earliest technologies were simple tools, such as stones and sticks, used for hunting and gathering. These technologies gradually became more advanced, with the development of agriculture leading to the creation of plows and other farming tools. The Industrial Revolution of the 18th and 19th centuries marked a significant turning point in the history of technology, with the development of steam power, machines, and factories transforming the way goods were produced and society was organized.

The 20th century saw the rapid development of electronics, with the invention of the radio, television, and eventually the computer. The internet, which emerged in the 1990s, marked a major turning point in the history of technology, connecting people and information around the world and ushering in the era of digital technology.

The impact of technology on society has been both positive and negative. On the positive side, technology has enabled people to communicate and connect in ways that were once impossible, improving social and economic outcomes. It has also led to significant advances in fields such as medicine, transportation, and energy production, improving the quality of life for people around the world.

However, technology has also had negative impacts on society, particularly in the areas of privacy and inequality. The increasing use of digital technology has raised concerns about data privacy and security, with individuals' personal information vulnerable to theft and misuse. Technology has also contributed to rising income inequality, with some people benefiting greatly from technological advances while others are left behind.

Despite these challenges, the evolution of technology has also given rise to the concept of minimalism, which emphasizes simplicity and efficiency in the use of technology. By focusing on the essential functions of technology and minimizing unnecessary complexity, minimalism can help address some of the negative impacts of technology on society. By using technology in a more mindful and intentional way, people can enjoy its benefits while minimizing its negative impacts on society and the environment.

regarding the topic "Chapter 1: The History of Technology and Minimalism" and refer to the revised or final outline, please write the content (for readers as normal people) for

"The emergence of minimalism in tech" the sub topic for about 3000 words long

As technology continued to evolve and become increasingly integrated into our lives, some people began to question whether this was really a good thing. They noticed that many of the products and services we use on a daily basis are designed to be addictive, keeping us hooked and constantly coming back for more. They also observed that our constant use of technology can have negative effects on our mental health and overall wellbeing.

This dissatisfaction with the state of technology led to the emergence of the minimalist movement in tech. Minimalism is all about simplifying your life by focusing on what's really important and getting rid of anything that doesn't add value. When applied to technology, minimalism means using only the tools and services that are truly necessary and avoiding anything that distracts or detracts from our quality of life.

The minimalist tech movement began to gain traction in the early 2000s, with people experimenting with different ways to simplify their digital lives. This included everything from decluttering their email inboxes and social media accounts to deleting apps and turning off notifications. The goal was to create a more intentional and mindful relationship with technology, one that didn't leave them feeling overwhelmed and stressed out.

Over time, the minimalist tech movement has grown and evolved. Today, there are countless blogs, podcasts, and social media accounts dedicated to the topic, and more and more people are embracing minimalism as a way to improve their relationship with technology. Minimalism in tech has become a way to push back against the forces of constant distraction and information overload, and to reclaim control over our digital lives.

But it's not just individuals who are adopting minimalist tech practices. Some companies are also starting to see the value in creating products and services that are intentionally minimalist. By designing tools and apps that are simple and easy to use, they're able to appeal to a growing segment of consumers who are looking for a more mindful and intentional relationship with technology.

Ultimately, the emergence of minimalism in tech represents a shift in our attitudes towards technology. Rather than blindly accepting the latest gadgets and services that are pushed on us, we're starting to question what truly adds value to our lives and what doesn't. By embracing minimalism, we're able to create a more intentional and mindful relationship with technology, one that supports our wellbeing and helps us to live a more fulfilling life.

The benefits of minimalism in tech historically
Minimalism in technology has a long history dating back to the early days of computing. One of the earliest examples of minimalism in tech is the UNIX operating system, which was developed in the 1960s by a group of programmers at Bell Labs. UNIX was designed to be a minimalist operating system that could run on a variety of hardware platforms. Its minimal design made it highly portable and efficient, and it quickly became popular in academic and research circles.

In the 1980s, Apple Computer introduced the Macintosh, which was a groundbreaking computer that featured a minimalist design. The Macintosh was designed to be easy to use, with a simple graphical user interface that allowed users to perform tasks without needing to know complex commands. This was a stark contrast to other computers of the time, which required users to enter commands in a command-line interface.

One of the biggest benefits of minimalism in tech is that it can lead to increased efficiency and productivity. By eliminating unnecessary features and focusing on the essentials, minimalist tech can be faster and more reliable than more complex systems. This was one of the key advantages of UNIX, which was able to run on a variety of hardware platforms and was highly efficient.

Another benefit of minimalism in tech is that it can lead to a better user experience. By focusing on the essentials and eliminating clutter, minimalist tech can be easier to use and more intuitive. This was one of the key advantages of the Macintosh, which was able to make computing accessible to a wider audience by simplifying the user interface.

Minimalism in tech has also played an important role in the development of the internet. The early days of the internet were characterized by simple, text-based interfaces that were easy to use and navigate. This minimal design was key to the success of early internet services like email and bulletin board systems, which were able to reach a wide audience due to their simplicity and ease of use.

Finally, minimalism in tech has played an important role in the development of mobile devices. The first smartphones were characterized by minimalist designs that focused on the essentials. This approach has continued to be important in the development of modern smartphones, which are designed to be simple and intuitive to use.

Overall, the history of technology has been marked by many examples of minimalism in tech, which have led to increased efficiency, better user experiences, and the development of new technologies. By focusing on the essentials and eliminating clutter, minimalist tech has played an important role in shaping the way we use technology today.

The drawbacks and criticisms of minimalism in tech
Minimalism in technology has its benefits, but it also has its drawbacks and criticisms. Some of these drawbacks and criticisms include:

1. Limited Functionality: One of the main criticisms of minimalism in technology is that it limits the functionality of devices and software. In order to achieve minimalism, features and functions are often removed or simplified, which can make devices less useful for certain tasks.

2. Lack of Innovation: Some critics argue that minimalism in technology can stifle innovation. By focusing on simplicity and functionality, minimalism may discourage developers from exploring new and creative ideas.

3. Limited Appeal: Minimalist designs may not appeal to everyone, and some users may prefer devices or software with more features and customization options.

4. Difficulty in Implementation: Implementing minimalism in technology can be challenging, as it requires careful consideration of which features are essential and which can

be removed or simplified. This process can be time-consuming and may require significant changes to the design and development process.

5. Incompatibility: Minimalist designs may not be compatible with certain types of users or use cases. For example, minimalist software may not be suitable for professional use or for users with specific accessibility needs.

Despite these criticisms, minimalism in technology remains a popular and effective approach for many users and developers. By focusing on simplicity and functionality, minimalism can help reduce clutter, increase efficiency, and improve the user experience. It is important, however, to consider the potential drawbacks and limitations of minimalism and to carefully evaluate whether it is the right approach for a particular project or device.

Chapter 2: The Basics of Blockchain

Understanding the fundamentals of blockchain technology

Blockchain is a distributed ledger technology that allows for secure, transparent, and tamper-proof record-keeping. At its core, it is a decentralized database that maintains a continuously growing list of records, called blocks, which are linked and secured using cryptography.

To understand blockchain technology, it's helpful to think of it as a digital ledger that keeps track of all transactions in a network. The ledger is maintained by a network of nodes, which are computers that are connected to the network. Each node has a copy of the ledger, and when a new transaction occurs, it is broadcast to all nodes in the network.

When a node receives a new transaction, it verifies its authenticity and then adds it to a block. Each block contains a set of transactions, along with a unique digital signature, called a hash, that identifies the block and links it to the previous block in the chain. This creates an unbreakable chain of blocks, hence the name "blockchain."

One of the key features of blockchain technology is its decentralization. There is no central authority that controls the blockchain, and all transactions are processed by the network of nodes. This means that there is no need for intermediaries, such as banks or other financial institutions, to verify and process transactions. This can lead to faster and cheaper transactions, as well as increased security and transparency.

Another important aspect of blockchain technology is its security. Because each block is linked to the previous block using cryptography, it is virtually impossible to tamper with the records in the blockchain. This makes blockchain technology ideal for applications where security and trust are paramount, such as financial transactions, supply chain management, and voting systems.

In summary, blockchain technology is a distributed ledger technology that allows for secure, transparent, and tamper-proof record-keeping. Its key features include decentralization, security, and transparency, which make it well-suited for a variety of applications.

The benefits and limitations of blockchain

Blockchain technology is being hailed as one of the most important technological innovations of our time. It has the potential to revolutionize the way we do business, govern, and interact with each other online. But like any technology, it comes with its own set of benefits and limitations.

Let's start with the benefits. One of the biggest advantages of blockchain is that it is a decentralized system. This means that there is no central authority that controls the flow of data or transactions. Instead, all participants in the network have a copy of the same ledger and work together to validate transactions. This creates a level of transparency and accountability that is hard to achieve with traditional centralized systems.

Another benefit of blockchain is its security. The technology uses cryptographic algorithms to ensure that data is kept secure and cannot be tampered with. This makes it virtually impossible for hackers to attack the system and steal data or funds. Additionally, because all participants in the network have a copy of the same ledger, it becomes very difficult to manipulate or corrupt data.

Blockchain technology is also incredibly efficient. Transactions can be processed much faster and at a lower cost than traditional methods, such as wire transfers or credit card transactions. This is because there are no intermediaries involved in the process, which reduces transaction fees and processing times.

However, blockchain technology also has its limitations. One of the biggest challenges facing blockchain is scalability. Currently, most blockchain networks can only handle a limited number of transactions per second. This makes it difficult to use the technology for high-volume applications, such as global payment systems.

Another limitation of blockchain is its complexity. The technology is still in its early stages, and many people find it difficult to understand. This can make it challenging for businesses and governments to adopt and implement the technology.

Finally, there are concerns about the environmental impact of blockchain. The process of verifying transactions on a blockchain network requires a lot of computational power, which can be very energy-intensive. As more and more people start using blockchain technology, there are concerns about the carbon footprint of the technology.

Overall, blockchain technology has a lot of potential to transform the way we do business and interact with each other online. But like any technology, it comes with its own set of benefits and limitations. It is up to us to carefully consider these factors and decide how best to use blockchain to create a more efficient, secure, and transparent world.

The relationship between minimalism and blockchain

In recent years, minimalism has become a popular concept in the world of blockchain technology. Minimalism in this context refers to the idea of designing blockchain systems that are simple, efficient, and effective in meeting their intended purpose.

One of the primary benefits of minimalism in blockchain is improved scalability. Blockchain systems that are designed with a minimalist approach can handle large volumes of transactions while maintaining high speeds and low costs. By minimizing the complexity of the system, blockchain developers can reduce the processing time required to validate transactions, resulting in faster processing times.

Another benefit of minimalism in blockchain is increased security. By simplifying the blockchain system, developers can eliminate unnecessary features that can introduce vulnerabilities. A minimalist blockchain system reduces the attack surface and makes it more difficult for attackers to exploit any weaknesses.

Furthermore, minimalism in blockchain has the potential to increase decentralization. By minimizing the number of nodes required to validate transactions, a blockchain system can become more accessible to a wider range of users. This can help to prevent the centralization of power that can occur when a small number of nodes control the majority of the network.

Despite these benefits, there are also some limitations to minimalism in blockchain. For example, a minimalist approach may not be suitable for all types of blockchain applications. Some applications may require more complex features that cannot be achieved through a minimalist design. Additionally, minimalism may not always be the most efficient approach, as some features may need to be added to meet the specific needs of a particular application.

Despite these limitations, the relationship between minimalism and blockchain is an important one. By adopting a minimalist approach to blockchain development, developers can create systems that are more efficient, secure, and accessible. As blockchain technology continues to evolve, it is likely that we will see more emphasis on minimalism and its role in shaping the future of this important technology.

Real-world applications of blockchain technology
Blockchain technology has gained a lot of attention in recent years due to its potential to transform various industries. Here are some real-world applications of blockchain technology:

1. Cryptocurrencies: Cryptocurrencies are digital currencies that use blockchain technology to enable secure, decentralized transactions. Bitcoin, the first and most popular cryptocurrency, is built on blockchain technology. Other cryptocurrencies, such as Ethereum and Litecoin, also use blockchain technology.

2. Supply chain management: Blockchain technology can be used to track products from their origin to the final destination, providing an immutable record of every transaction along the way. This can be used to ensure the

authenticity and quality of products, as well as to reduce the risk of fraud and counterfeiting.

3. Voting systems: Blockchain technology can be used to create secure, transparent, and tamper-proof voting systems. By using blockchain technology, it is possible to create a voting system that is immune to fraud, hacking, and other forms of tampering.

4. Healthcare: Blockchain technology can be used to securely store and share medical records, enabling patients to have complete control over their medical data. This can be particularly useful in emergency situations where quick access to medical records can be critical.

5. Banking and finance: Blockchain technology can be used to create a more secure and transparent financial system. By using blockchain technology, it is possible to create a system where transactions are recorded and verified in a decentralized and transparent way, reducing the risk of fraud and increasing trust in the financial system.

6. Identity verification: Blockchain technology can be used to create secure and tamper-proof digital identities. By using blockchain technology, it is possible to create a system where individuals have complete control over their digital identity, reducing the risk of identity theft and fraud.

7. Real estate: Blockchain technology can be used to create a more transparent and efficient real estate market. By using blockchain technology, it is possible to create a system where real estate transactions are recorded and verified in a decentralized and transparent way, reducing the risk of fraud and increasing trust in the real estate market.

These are just a few examples of the real-world applications of blockchain technology. As the technology continues to evolve, it is likely that we will see more and more innovative uses of blockchain technology in various industries.

Chapter 3: The Basics of AI

Understanding the fundamentals of AI technology

Artificial intelligence, or AI, is a rapidly advancing field of computer science that involves developing machines that can perform tasks that typically require human intelligence. At its core, AI is about creating algorithms and systems that can analyze data, recognize patterns, and make decisions based on that information.

One of the key features of AI is its ability to learn and improve over time. This is done through the use of machine learning algorithms, which enable the system to adapt and improve its performance based on feedback from the data it processes.

AI technology is typically divided into two main categories: narrow or weak AI, and general or strong AI. Narrow AI is designed to perform specific tasks, such as playing chess or recognizing images. General AI, on the other hand, is intended to be more versatile and adaptable, with the ability to learn and reason across a wide range of tasks and contexts.

There are many different applications for AI technology, ranging from voice assistants like Siri and Alexa to self-driving cars and advanced medical diagnostic tools. As the field continues to advance, it is likely that we will see AI systems playing an increasingly important role in many areas of our lives. However, there are also concerns about the potential risks and drawbacks of this technology, such as the risk of job displacement and the ethical considerations around the use of AI in decision-making processes.

Overall, AI is a complex and rapidly evolving field with many exciting possibilities and challenges. As with any technology, it is important to approach it with caution and to carefully consider its potential benefits and risks.

The benefits and limitations of AI

Artificial Intelligence (AI) is a field of computer science that aims to create intelligent machines that can perform tasks that would typically require human intelligence, such as visual perception, speech recognition, decision-making, and natural language processing. AI has become increasingly prevalent in various industries, including healthcare, finance, transportation, and entertainment. The benefits of AI are numerous and diverse, but it also poses several limitations and challenges.

One of the main benefits of AI is its ability to automate routine tasks and streamline operations, thereby saving time and reducing costs. For instance, chatbots powered by AI technology can be used in customer service to answer common queries and resolve issues, freeing up human agents to focus on more complex tasks. AI can also be used in healthcare to analyze medical records and identify potential health risks, allowing doctors to provide personalized treatment plans for their patients.

AI technology also has the potential to improve safety and security, for instance, by detecting and preventing cyber attacks and fraud. AI-powered autonomous vehicles can also reduce human error in driving and decrease the number of road accidents. Additionally, AI technology can enhance scientific research by analyzing large datasets and identifying patterns that humans may not be able to detect.

However, AI also has some limitations and challenges that need to be addressed. One of the main limitations of AI is its reliance on large datasets, which can be biased and incomplete. This can result in the AI system making inaccurate predictions or decisions. There is also a risk of AI technology being used for malicious purposes, such as cyber attacks or data breaches. Furthermore, the increasing automation of tasks through AI may lead to job displacement and social inequality.

To address these limitations and challenges, researchers and policymakers need to work together to ensure that AI technology is developed and used ethically and responsibly. This includes ensuring that AI systems are transparent and accountable, and that they are designed to mitigate the risk of bias and errors. Additionally, policymakers should consider the potential impact of AI on employment and work towards creating new job opportunities that are not susceptible to automation.

In summary, AI technology has numerous benefits and applications, but it also poses several challenges and limitations. By addressing these challenges and ensuring that AI is developed and used responsibly, we can maximize the benefits of this technology while minimizing its potential risks.

The relationship between minimalism and AI

Artificial intelligence (AI) and minimalism may seem like two unrelated concepts, but they are actually closely connected in many ways. In this chapter, we will explore the relationship between minimalism and AI.

To start, let's define minimalism. Minimalism is a lifestyle philosophy that emphasizes living with less, simplifying one's life, and removing excess. It's about focusing on what's essential and removing distractions that don't add value to one's life.

When it comes to AI, minimalism can be applied in a few different ways. One way is through the development of minimalist AI algorithms. These algorithms are designed to be simple and efficient, with the goal of achieving high performance with minimal computational resources. By keeping the algorithms simple, they can be easier to understand, debug, and maintain. Minimalist AI algorithms can be particularly useful in resource-constrained environments, such as mobile devices, where power and computational resources are limited.

Another way that minimalism and AI are related is through the application of minimalist design principles to AI systems. Minimalist design emphasizes simplicity, clarity, and functionality. By applying minimalist design principles to AI systems, designers can create interfaces that are intuitive and easy to use. This is particularly important in applications such as virtual assistants or chatbots, where users expect a seamless and intuitive experience.

Minimalism can also be applied to the ethical considerations surrounding AI. As AI becomes increasingly powerful and ubiquitous, there is a growing concern about the potential negative impacts it could have on society. One way to mitigate these risks is through a minimalist approach to AI development. This means focusing on developing AI systems that are designed to be transparent, trustworthy, and aligned with human values. By keeping the goals of AI development simple and focused on human needs, we can help ensure that AI is developed in a way that benefits society as a whole.

However, there are also potential drawbacks to a minimalist approach to AI. One concern is that minimalist AI algorithms may not be as accurate or powerful as more complex ones. In some cases, a more complex algorithm may be necessary to achieve the desired level of performance. Additionally, there is a risk that a minimalist approach could lead to oversimplification of complex problems, which could result in unintended consequences.

In conclusion, while there are both benefits and drawbacks to a minimalist approach to AI, the two concepts are closely related. By applying minimalist principles to AI development, we can create systems that are efficient, intuitive, and aligned with human values. However, it's important to recognize that there may be cases where a more complex approach is necessary to achieve the desired level of performance. Ultimately, the goal should be to develop AI systems that are both powerful and responsible, with a focus on benefiting society as a whole.

Real-world applications of AI technology

Artificial intelligence (AI) is one of the most rapidly growing fields of technology today, with applications in almost every industry imaginable. In this chapter, we will explore the real-world applications of AI, including some of the most innovative and impactful uses of this technology.

1. Healthcare: AI has the potential to revolutionize healthcare, with applications such as personalized medicine, drug discovery, and medical image analysis. Personalized medicine involves using AI algorithms to analyze a patient's genetic makeup and medical history to create personalized treatment plans. Drug discovery involves using AI to analyze vast amounts of data and identify potential new drug

candidates. Medical image analysis uses AI algorithms to analyze medical images, such as X-rays and MRIs, to help doctors diagnose and treat patients.

2. Financial services: AI is being used in the financial industry to automate processes such as fraud detection, risk assessment, and trading. For example, AI algorithms can analyze large amounts of data to identify patterns and anomalies that could indicate fraudulent activity. AI is also being used in trading to analyze market data and make predictions about future market trends.

3. Transportation: Self-driving cars are perhaps the most well-known application of AI in transportation. However, AI is also being used to optimize traffic flow, reduce congestion, and improve public transportation. For example, AI algorithms can analyze real-time traffic data to identify the most efficient routes for public transportation.

4. Retail: AI is being used in the retail industry to improve the customer experience and increase sales. For example, AI algorithms can analyze customer data to create personalized recommendations and offers. AI-powered chatbots are also being used to provide customer service and support.

5. Manufacturing: AI is being used in manufacturing to optimize processes and increase efficiency. For example, AI algorithms can analyze sensor data to identify potential

equipment failures before they occur. AI is also being used to optimize supply chains and reduce waste.

6. Education: AI is being used in education to personalize learning and improve student outcomes. For example, AI-powered tutoring systems can analyze student data to identify areas where a student needs additional support and provide personalized recommendations. AI is also being used to analyze student data to identify factors that contribute to academic success.

7. Entertainment: AI is being used in the entertainment industry to create personalized experiences for consumers. For example, streaming services are using AI algorithms to analyze user data and make recommendations for content based on their viewing history.

Overall, AI has the potential to transform almost every industry and aspect of our lives. While there are certainly limitations and challenges to be addressed, the potential benefits of AI make it an exciting and rapidly evolving field to watch.

Chapter 4: The Minimalist Approach to Tech

The principles of minimalist tech

The minimalist approach to tech is centered around the idea of simplifying and decluttering one's digital life. By reducing the number of devices, apps, and digital distractions, individuals can focus on what truly matters and enhance their overall well-being.

Here are some of the principles of minimalist tech:

1. Intentionality: The first principle of minimalist tech is being intentional about what you choose to keep in your digital life. This means taking the time to evaluate whether each app, device, or service is essential and adds value to your life. By intentionally selecting the digital tools you use, you can avoid the unnecessary clutter that can overwhelm and distract you.

2. Simplicity: A minimalist approach to tech values simplicity and ease of use. This means choosing digital tools that are straightforward and uncomplicated, with minimal features and distractions. Simple tech allows you to focus on what's important and reduces the cognitive load that comes with using complex systems.

3. Quality over quantity: In minimalist tech, quality is valued over quantity. Instead of having multiple devices that serve similar purposes, or using a plethora of apps that do the same thing, minimalist tech focuses on high-quality tools that serve a specific purpose well.

4. Mindfulness: Being mindful of how you use technology is an important principle of minimalist tech. This means

paying attention to how much time you spend on your devices, and being present in the moment rather than getting lost in digital distractions. By using technology with intention and awareness, you can cultivate a healthier relationship with digital tools and avoid the negative consequences of excessive use.

5. Sustainability: A minimalist approach to tech also values sustainability. This means choosing devices and services that are environmentally friendly and have a minimal impact on the planet. By reducing your digital footprint, you can contribute to a more sustainable future.

Overall, the principles of minimalist tech aim to help individuals use technology in a way that enhances their lives and well-being, rather than detracting from it. By intentionally selecting high-quality digital tools that are simple and sustainable, individuals can create a more mindful and fulfilling relationship with technology.

Strategies for implementing minimalism in tech
Now that we understand the principles of minimalist tech, the question arises: how can we implement minimalism in our daily use of technology? Below are some strategies for incorporating minimalist principles into our tech habits.

1. Evaluate your current tech usage: The first step towards minimalism is to evaluate your current tech usage. Take stock of the devices you use, the apps you have installed, and the websites you visit. Identify the ones you use the most and the ones you can do without.

2. Eliminate the unnecessary: Once you've identified the apps, devices, and websites you use the least, it's time to eliminate them. Uninstall apps you rarely use and unsubscribe from newsletters and notifications that you don't find useful.

3. Simplify your devices: Consider simplifying your tech devices by opting for ones that serve multiple purposes. For example, instead of having a separate device for music, a separate device for email, and a separate device for web browsing, opt for a tablet or laptop that can handle all of these tasks.

4. Prioritize privacy: Minimalism in tech also means prioritizing your privacy. Review the privacy policies of the apps and websites you use and opt for ones that collect less data or offer more control over your data.

5. Embrace analog alternatives: Sometimes, the best way to implement minimalism in tech is to embrace analog alternatives. For example, instead of using a digital to-do list app, consider using a physical notebook. Instead of listening

to music on a streaming service, consider buying vinyl records.

6. Set boundaries: Finally, set boundaries for yourself when it comes to tech usage. Create designated tech-free zones in your home, such as the bedroom or dining table. Set aside specific times of the day for checking email and social media, and avoid checking them outside of those times.

By incorporating these strategies into your tech habits, you can adopt a more minimalist approach to technology and reap the benefits that come with it. Not only will you experience less stress and distraction, but you'll also have more time and mental space for the things that matter most in your life.

The benefits of a minimalist tech approach

As we have discussed earlier, adopting a minimalist approach to technology can bring numerous benefits to our lives. In this section, we will delve deeper into these benefits and how they can make a significant impact on our daily routines.

1. Increased Productivity: Minimalism in tech can help us stay focused on our tasks and minimize distractions. By limiting the number of apps, notifications, and gadgets, we can free up mental space and achieve more in less time.

2. Improved Mental Health: Excessive use of technology can have adverse effects on our mental health, such as anxiety, stress, and depression. By reducing our screen time and creating boundaries around our tech usage, we can improve our overall well-being and have more time for self-care.

3. Enhanced Creativity: Minimalism in tech can help us tap into our creative potential. By eliminating distractions and spending more time in solitude, we can give our minds the freedom to explore new ideas and generate innovative solutions.

4. Better Relationships: Spending too much time on our screens can negatively impact our relationships with friends and family. By reducing our dependence on technology, we can focus on building meaningful connections and improving our communication skills.

5. Reduced Environmental Impact: The production and disposal of technology have a significant environmental impact. By embracing a minimalist approach to tech, we can reduce our carbon footprint and contribute to a more sustainable future.

6. Financial Benefits: Technology can be expensive, and a minimalist approach can help us save money by focusing on essential gadgets and services. By avoiding unnecessary

upgrades and subscriptions, we can reduce our expenses and increase our financial stability.

Overall, adopting a minimalist approach to technology can have a positive impact on various aspects of our lives. By prioritizing what truly matters and focusing on what adds value, we can lead more intentional and fulfilling lives.

Examples of companies and individuals who practice minimalist tech

Minimalism in technology has gained popularity among individuals and companies alike. Many are realizing the benefits of minimizing tech usage and finding ways to incorporate it into their daily lives and work. In this chapter, we will explore examples of companies and individuals who practice minimalist tech.

1. Apple Apple is one of the most well-known companies that have adopted minimalist principles in their products. From their hardware design to software features, they strive for simplicity and ease of use. The minimalist design of their products has garnered them a massive following, and their products are highly sought after.

2. Google Google is another company that has embraced minimalist principles in their products. They have streamlined their search engine to provide users with the

most relevant information quickly. They have also created a minimalist interface for their email service, Gmail, which has made it incredibly popular among users.

3. Tesla Tesla is a car company that has gained massive popularity for their electric vehicles. Their cars are known for their sleek, minimalist design and innovative features. Tesla's CEO, Elon Musk, is also known for his minimalist approach to life and work, which has contributed to the company's success.

4. Marie Kondo Marie Kondo is a Japanese organizing consultant and author who has gained a massive following for her minimalist approach to decluttering and organizing. Her method, known as the KonMari method, involves keeping only the items that spark joy in a person's life and getting rid of the rest. Her approach has inspired people to simplify their lives and reduce clutter.

5. Tim Ferriss Tim Ferriss is an American author, entrepreneur, and podcaster who has embraced minimalism in his work and personal life. He is known for his book, "The 4-Hour Work Week," which encourages people to focus on the most important tasks and eliminate unnecessary work. He also advocates for simplifying personal possessions and reducing clutter to increase productivity and reduce stress.

6. Leo Babauta Leo Babauta is a blogger and author who has gained a massive following for his blog, "Zen Habits." He advocates for a minimalist lifestyle and provides practical tips for simplifying various aspects of life, including work, relationships, and personal possessions. His approach has inspired many people to live a more intentional and fulfilling life.

7. Joshua Fields Millburn and Ryan Nicodemus Joshua Fields Millburn and Ryan Nicodemus are the founders of the Minimalists, a popular blog, podcast, and documentary series that promotes a minimalist lifestyle. They encourage people to question their possessions and focus on the things that truly matter in life. Their approach has resonated with many people who are seeking a simpler and more intentional life.

In conclusion, minimalist tech principles have been adopted by many individuals and companies who are seeking a simpler, more intentional way of living and working. These examples show that minimalist tech can be applied to various aspects of life and work, and can lead to increased productivity, reduced stress, and greater fulfillment.

Chapter 5: Mindful Consumption in the Digital Age
The impact of digital consumption on the environment

In today's digital age, we are constantly consuming information, entertainment, and products through our digital devices such as smartphones, laptops, and tablets. However, the convenience of digital consumption comes with an environmental cost. This chapter will explore the impact of digital consumption on the environment and the steps we can take to reduce our digital carbon footprint.

Energy Consumption One of the biggest impacts of digital consumption on the environment is the energy consumption required to power the devices we use. Data centers that store and process our digital information consume a significant amount of energy. According to a 2019 report by the International Energy Agency (IEA), data centers accounted for 1% of global electricity consumption and 0.3% of global CO_2 emissions, a figure that is expected to triple by 2030.

In addition to data centers, the energy required to manufacture and transport digital devices also contributes to their environmental impact. According to a report by the European Environmental Bureau (EEB), the manufacturing of a single smartphone requires approximately 14 kg of CO_2 emissions, which is equivalent to the amount of CO_2 produced by driving a car for 100 km.

E-waste Another environmental impact of digital consumption is e-waste. E-waste refers to the disposal of electronic devices, which can contain hazardous materials such as lead, mercury, and cadmium. According to a 2019 report by the United Nations, the world produced 53.6 million metric tons of e-waste, and only 17.4% of it was recycled. The rest ended up in landfills or was illegally traded, causing harm to the environment and human health.

Internet Overload The constant consumption of digital content also contributes to internet overload. The more people consume and share digital content, the more strain it puts on the internet infrastructure. This can lead to slower internet speeds, and the need to build more data centers to keep up with the demand.

Reducing Your Digital Carbon Footprint While digital consumption may seem unavoidable, there are steps we can take to reduce our digital carbon footprint. One way is to use digital devices and services more mindfully. This means being aware of the energy consumption required for the devices and services we use and minimizing our usage accordingly. For example, turning off devices when not in use, using energy-efficient settings, and reducing screen time.

Another way to reduce our digital carbon footprint is to choose more sustainable devices and services. This includes selecting devices with a longer lifespan, buying second-hand devices, and choosing services that use renewable energy sources.

Finally, recycling electronic devices properly can help reduce e-waste. Many countries and organizations have e-waste recycling programs in place that can help ensure that electronic devices are disposed of safely and sustainably.

Conclusion The impact of digital consumption on the environment is significant, and it's up to each of us to take responsibility for our digital carbon footprint. By using digital devices and services more mindfully, choosing more sustainable options, and properly recycling electronic devices, we can reduce our environmental impact and work towards a more sustainable digital future.

The benefits of mindful consumption in tech

The digital age has brought with it countless benefits and conveniences, but it has also given rise to new problems, such as the negative impact of digital consumption on our well-being and the environment. However, there is a growing movement towards mindful consumption in tech, which focuses on being intentional about our use of technology in order to reduce our impact and improve our lives. In this section, we will explore the benefits of mindful consumption in tech.

1. Reduced Environmental Impact

One of the most significant benefits of mindful consumption in tech is a reduced environmental impact. The production, use, and disposal of electronic devices contribute to environmental problems such as pollution, resource depletion, and greenhouse gas emissions. By being mindful of our tech consumption, we can reduce our overall impact on the environment.

For example, we can:

- Choose to repair or refurbish our devices instead of buying new ones
- Opt for energy-efficient devices and power-saving settings
- Use digital products and services that prioritize sustainability and ethical practices
- Recycle or dispose of electronic devices properly, rather than contributing to e-waste

2. Improved Well-being

Another benefit of mindful consumption in tech is improved well-being. The constant use of technology can have negative effects on our mental health, such as increased stress, anxiety, and addiction. By being more intentional about our tech use, we can reduce these negative effects and improve our overall well-being.

For example, we can:

- Set boundaries and limits on our tech use, such as designated screen-free times and places

- Use mindfulness techniques to reduce stress and increase self-awareness

- Choose digital products and services that prioritize user privacy and well-being

- Prioritize face-to-face communication and social interaction over digital communication

3. Increased Productivity and Focus

Mindful consumption in tech can also lead to increased productivity and focus. The constant distraction and interruptions of technology can make it difficult to concentrate and get things done. By being intentional about our tech use, we can reduce distractions and increase our ability to focus on important tasks.

For example, we can:

- Turn off notifications and limit our use of social media and other distracting apps

- Use productivity tools and apps that help us stay organized and focused

- Take breaks and prioritize self-care to avoid burnout and exhaustion

- Choose digital products and services that prioritize simplicity and functionality over excess features and distractions

In conclusion, mindful consumption in tech has many benefits, including a reduced environmental impact, improved well-being, and increased productivity and focus. By being intentional about our use of technology and prioritizing our values, we can create a healthier and more sustainable relationship with technology.

Strategies for reducing digital consumption

In today's fast-paced digital world, it's easy to get lost in the endless sea of notifications, emails, and social media feeds. Many people find themselves spending hours mindlessly scrolling through their screens, often at the expense of their mental health, productivity, and overall well-being. The good news is that there are several strategies that you can adopt to reduce your digital consumption and reclaim your time and energy. Here are some effective ways to get started:

1. Set Boundaries

The first step to reducing digital consumption is to set boundaries. This means being intentional about the time and space you allocate to technology. One way to do this is to establish a tech-free zone in your home or workplace, such as your bedroom or dining area. Another way is to set specific times of the day when you will check your email, social media, or other apps. For example, you could check your email only twice a day, once in the morning and once in the afternoon, and avoid checking it outside those designated times.

2. Turn Off Notifications

Notifications can be a major distraction and can interrupt your work, conversations, or leisure time. To reduce digital consumption, consider turning off notifications for non-essential apps or turning off your phone altogether during certain times of the day. This way, you can focus on the task at hand without being constantly bombarded by alerts and updates.

3. Practice Mindful Consumption

Mindful consumption means being intentional about what you consume online and how much time you spend doing it. This involves being aware of your browsing habits and consciously choosing to engage with content that is meaningful and relevant to your goals and interests. To practice mindful consumption, ask yourself before clicking on a link or scrolling through a feed, "Is this adding value to my life? Is this something I truly need to see or read?"

4. Digital Detox

Sometimes, the best way to reduce digital consumption is to take a break from technology altogether. A digital detox involves unplugging from all devices and screens for a designated period, such as a day, weekend, or week. During this time, you can focus on other activities that bring you joy and fulfillment, such as spending time in nature, reading a book, or spending quality time with friends and family.

5. Use Technology to Your Advantage

While reducing digital consumption is important, it's also important to remember that technology can be a useful tool when used intentionally. To make technology work for you, consider using productivity apps that help you stay organized and focused, or meditation apps that help you manage stress and improve your mental health. By using technology in a mindful way, you can enhance your productivity, creativity, and overall well-being.

6. Develop a Support System

Reducing digital consumption can be challenging, especially if you're used to being constantly connected. To make the process easier, consider developing a support system, such as a group of friends or family members who are also committed to reducing their digital consumption. You can hold each other accountable, share tips and strategies, and provide encouragement and motivation.

In conclusion, reducing digital consumption is an important aspect of mindful consumption in the digital age. By setting boundaries, turning off notifications, practicing mindful consumption, taking a digital detox, using technology to your advantage, and developing a support system, you can reduce your digital consumption and enhance your overall well-being.

The relationship between mindful consumption and minimalism in tech

In recent years, the concepts of minimalism and mindful consumption have gained traction as people become more aware of the impact of their daily choices on the environment and their own well-being. These two concepts intersect in the realm of technology, where individuals are seeking ways to reduce their digital consumption while still enjoying the benefits of technology.

Minimalism in tech emphasizes simplicity and functionality, and this approach can also be applied to mindful consumption. When we become more mindful of our technology usage, we can identify what is truly essential and eliminate the excess that clutters our digital lives. This, in turn, reduces our overall digital consumption.

Here are some ways in which mindful consumption and minimalism in tech are related:

1. Prioritizing what matters: Both minimalism in tech and mindful consumption involve prioritizing what truly matters to us. By focusing on what is important and necessary, we can reduce our consumption of digital content and technology.

2. Simplifying our technology usage: Minimalism in tech encourages us to simplify our digital lives by eliminating unnecessary apps, devices, and subscriptions. This approach also helps us to reduce our digital consumption by streamlining our technology usage.

3. Encouraging intentional technology use: Mindful consumption emphasizes the importance of intentional choices, and this can be applied to technology usage as well. By being more intentional with how we use technology, we can reduce our overall consumption while still benefiting from its many advantages.

4. Reducing distractions: Digital distractions can be a major source of wasted time and energy. Both minimalism in tech and mindful consumption encourage us to eliminate distractions and focus on what truly matters.

5. Promoting well-being: Mindful consumption and minimalism in tech both promote well-being by encouraging

us to be more intentional with our choices. By reducing our digital consumption and focusing on what truly matters, we can improve our overall well-being and quality of life.

In essence, mindful consumption and minimalism in tech are two sides of the same coin. By combining these two approaches, we can reduce our digital consumption while still benefiting from the many advantages that technology offers. Ultimately, this approach allows us to live more intentionally and mindfully, leading to a more fulfilling and sustainable lifestyle.

Chapter 6: The Ethics of Technology

The ethical considerations of technology

Technology has become an integral part of our lives, and with its increasing role comes the need to consider the ethical implications of its use. There are a variety of ethical considerations that arise in the context of technology, from privacy and security concerns to the impact of technology on society and the environment. In this chapter, we will explore some of the key ethical considerations of technology and what they mean for individuals and society as a whole.

Privacy and Security One of the most significant ethical considerations of technology is privacy and security. As we share more and more of our personal information online, the risk of that information being compromised or misused also increases. For example, social media platforms and search engines collect vast amounts of data about their users, which can be used to target advertising or even manipulate individuals' beliefs and behaviors. Additionally, data breaches and cyberattacks can result in the theft of sensitive information, such as financial or healthcare data.

As technology continues to evolve, the need for strong privacy and security protections becomes more pressing. Individuals must be able to trust that their data is being handled responsibly and that they have control over how it is used. Companies and organizations also have a responsibility to protect their users' data and to be transparent about how that data is being used.

Impact on Society Another ethical consideration of technology is its impact on society. While technology has the potential to bring significant benefits, such as increased efficiency and access to information, it can also have negative consequences. For example, automation and artificial intelligence have the potential to eliminate jobs, leading to economic inequality and social unrest. Social media platforms can also contribute to the spread of misinformation and polarization, creating a more divided society.

It is important to consider the potential impact of technology on society as a whole, rather than simply focusing on individual benefits or drawbacks. This requires careful thought and consideration, as well as a willingness to make changes when necessary to ensure that technology is being used in a responsible and beneficial way.

Environmental Impact The environmental impact of technology is also an important ethical consideration. The production and disposal of electronic devices contribute to environmental problems such as pollution, resource depletion, and climate change. Additionally, the energy consumption of data centers and other technology infrastructure can be significant, contributing to greenhouse gas emissions and other environmental problems.

As technology continues to become more ubiquitous, it is important to consider its environmental impact and to take steps to mitigate its effects. This can include measures such as designing devices with longer lifespans, using more sustainable materials in production, and using renewable energy to power data centers.

Bias and Discrimination Finally, the potential for bias and discrimination in technology is another important ethical consideration. For example, algorithms used in hiring or loan decisions may be biased against certain groups, leading to unequal outcomes. Similarly, facial recognition technology has been shown to be less accurate when used on individuals with darker skin tones, leading to concerns about its potential use in law enforcement.

It is important to ensure that technology is designed and implemented in a way that is fair and unbiased. This may require addressing underlying social and economic inequalities, as well as carefully considering the potential impact of technology on marginalized groups.

Conclusion The ethical considerations of technology are complex and multifaceted, requiring careful thought and consideration. By being mindful of the potential impact of technology on privacy, society, the environment, and equality, individuals and organizations can work to ensure that technology is being used in a responsible and beneficial way. Ultimately, the ethical use of technology is essential for creating a more just and equitable society.

The role of minimalism in ethical tech

As we continue to develop and use technology in our daily lives, it's important to consider the ethical implications of these advancements. From data privacy concerns to the impact of technology on job displacement, ethical considerations are an integral part of the technology conversation.

One approach to promoting ethical technology is through the lens of minimalism. By embracing a minimalist approach, we can prioritize ethical considerations in the development and use of technology. Here are some ways in which minimalism can play a role in promoting ethical tech:

1. Simplifying technology: By embracing a minimalist approach, we can simplify technology and avoid unnecessary complexity. This can help reduce the potential for ethical issues such as data breaches or unintended consequences of technology use.

2. Promoting transparency: Minimalism encourages transparency in the development and use of technology. This means that companies should be upfront about their data collection practices and the intended use of data collected. This can help users make informed decisions about how their data is used and promote trust between users and tech companies.

3. Prioritizing user experience: A minimalist approach to technology puts the user first. This means creating technology that is intuitive, easy to use, and designed with the user in mind. This can help promote ethical use of

technology by making it more accessible and less intimidating for users.

4. Reducing waste: Minimalism encourages us to reduce waste in all aspects of our lives, including technology. This means considering the environmental impact of technology and striving to create products and services that are sustainable and environmentally responsible.

5. Encouraging ethical behavior: Finally, a minimalist approach to technology can encourage ethical behavior by promoting values such as simplicity, honesty, and transparency. This can create a culture of ethical tech use and help hold tech companies accountable for their actions.

While minimalism is not a silver bullet solution to all ethical considerations in technology, it can be a valuable tool in promoting ethical behavior and responsible use of technology. By prioritizing simplicity, transparency, and the user experience, we can create technology that is both useful and ethical.

Examples of ethical dilemmas in tech

Technology has transformed the way we live our lives, and as our reliance on technology increases, so do the ethical considerations that come with it. From privacy concerns to automation of jobs, there are numerous examples of ethical dilemmas that arise from the use of technology. In this section, we will explore some of the most notable ethical dilemmas in tech.

1. Data Privacy: One of the biggest ethical concerns with technology is data privacy. Tech companies collect vast amounts of data from users, including personal information, online behavior, and location data. This data is often used for targeted advertising or sold to third-party companies. The Cambridge Analytica scandal, in which millions of Facebook users had their data harvested without their consent, highlights the importance of protecting user data.

2. Algorithmic Bias: Machine learning algorithms are becoming increasingly popular in decision-making processes, from hiring to loan approvals. However, these algorithms can be biased, perpetuating discrimination against certain groups. For example, Amazon had to scrap its AI recruiting tool after it was found to be biased against women.

3. Automation of Jobs: The automation of jobs is another ethical dilemma in tech. As machines become more capable, there is a risk that many jobs will become obsolete, leaving people without work and without a source of income. This raises questions about the responsibility of tech companies to help workers transition to new industries.

4. Artificial Intelligence: As AI technology advances, it raises ethical questions about its use. For example, the use of autonomous weapons, such as drones, raises concerns about the ability to make ethical decisions in the absence of human intervention. There are also concerns about the use of AI for surveillance, which could be used to violate privacy rights.

5. Social Media: Social media platforms have given individuals a powerful voice, but they have also been used to spread hate speech and misinformation. Social media companies are grappling with how to balance free speech with the need to protect users from harmful content.

6. Cybersecurity: With the increasing amount of personal information being stored online, cybersecurity has become a major ethical concern. Companies have a responsibility to protect user data from hackers and cybercriminals, but they also have a responsibility to disclose data breaches to users in a timely and transparent manner.

7. Digital Divide: The digital divide refers to the gap between those who have access to technology and those who do not. As technology becomes more pervasive, there is a risk that those without access to technology will be left behind, exacerbating existing inequalities. Tech companies have a responsibility to address the digital divide by providing access to technology to marginalized communities.

In conclusion, technology has brought about many benefits, but it has also raised numerous ethical concerns. It is important for individuals and companies to consider the ethical implications of their use of technology and to work towards finding solutions to these challenges. By doing so, we can ensure that technology is used in a responsible and ethical way that benefits society as a whole.

Strategies for ethical tech practices

As technology continues to rapidly advance and become more integrated into our daily lives, it is important to consider the ethical implications of these developments. Ethical tech practices can help ensure that technology is used in a responsible and beneficial way that prioritizes the well-being of individuals and society as a whole. Here are some strategies for ethical tech practices:

1. Prioritize User Privacy: One of the most important ethical considerations in tech is the protection of user privacy. This can include implementing strong data security measures, being transparent about data collection and usage, and allowing users to control their own data. Companies and individuals should always consider the potential risks and benefits of collecting and sharing user data, and ensure that users are informed and consenting to the use of their data.

2. Foster Inclusivity and Diversity: Technology should be accessible and usable for all people, regardless of their background or abilities. Ethical tech practices should prioritize inclusivity and diversity, such as designing products and services that are user-friendly and accessible for people with disabilities or from different cultural backgrounds. Companies and individuals should also strive to eliminate bias and discrimination in the design and implementation of technology.

3. Ensure Transparency and Accountability: It is important for companies and individuals to be transparent about their use of technology, including how it is designed, developed, and used. Ethical tech practices should prioritize transparency and accountability, including being open about potential risks and benefits, and engaging in ongoing dialogue with stakeholders to ensure that technology is being used in a responsible and beneficial way.

4. Consider the Social and Environmental Impact: The use of technology can have significant social and environmental impacts, and ethical tech practices should consider these impacts when designing and using technology. This can include considering the environmental footprint of technology, such as its energy consumption and waste

generation, as well as the potential social impacts, such as the displacement of jobs or the amplification of inequalities.

5. Empower Users: Users should have control over the technology they use and be empowered to make informed decisions about how they engage with technology. Ethical tech practices should prioritize user empowerment, including providing users with information about their data and privacy, and allowing them to customize their experience and control their own data.

6. Embrace Minimalism: The minimalist approach to tech can also be a valuable strategy for ethical tech practices. By prioritizing simplicity and functionality, minimalist tech can reduce the potential for harmful or unethical uses of technology, and prioritize the well-being of users over profit or other incentives.

7. Engage in Ongoing Learning and Reflection: Technology is constantly evolving, and ethical tech practices should prioritize ongoing learning and reflection. This can include staying up-to-date on the latest developments in technology and their ethical implications, as well as engaging in ongoing reflection about the potential risks and benefits of technology use.

Overall, ethical tech practices should prioritize the well-being of individuals and society as a whole, and consider the potential social, environmental, and ethical impacts of technology use. By implementing these strategies, we can ensure that technology is used in a responsible and beneficial way that supports our collective well-being.

Chapter 7: The Future of Minimalist Tech

Emerging trends in minimalist tech

As technology continues to evolve, minimalist tech has emerged as a counter-movement to the overwhelming complexity and overconsumption of the digital age. Here are some emerging trends in minimalist tech that are shaping the future of technology:

1. Simplicity and Minimalism: As more people embrace minimalism and simplicity in their daily lives, technology is following suit. This trend is evidenced in the popularity of minimalist interfaces and design. Companies are shifting towards user-friendly and intuitive interfaces, which create a more streamlined and effortless user experience.

2. Sustainable Tech: Environmental consciousness is becoming increasingly important in the tech industry. Many companies are investing in green energy, recyclable materials, and other sustainable practices to reduce their carbon footprint. Consumers are also becoming more aware of the impact of their digital consumption on the

environment and are seeking out sustainable tech alternatives.

3. Digital Detox and Mindful Tech Use: The rise of digital addiction has prompted a movement towards mindful tech use and digital detoxing. Consumers are looking for ways to disconnect from technology and develop healthy relationships with their devices. Companies are developing tools and resources to help users manage their tech usage and cultivate more mindful habits.

4. Privacy and Security: As the amount of personal data being collected and shared online continues to grow, privacy and security are becoming more important concerns. Consumers are demanding greater control over their personal information and are seeking out tech products and services that prioritize privacy and security.

5. Ethical Tech: With the increasing influence of technology in our lives, ethical considerations are becoming more important. Companies are being held accountable for the impact of their products and services on society, and consumers are demanding more ethical tech solutions. This includes everything from transparency in data collection to responsible AI development.

6. Augmented Reality: Augmented reality (AR) is an emerging technology that integrates digital elements into the

real world. AR has the potential to create immersive and interactive experiences that can enhance productivity, education, and entertainment. Minimalist tech is exploring how AR can be used to enhance simplicity and minimalism in various fields.

7. Artificial Intelligence: Artificial intelligence (AI) has the potential to revolutionize how we interact with technology. Minimalist tech is exploring how AI can be used to create more efficient and intuitive interfaces and streamline complex tasks. However, ethical concerns surrounding AI development and usage must also be considered.

In conclusion, minimalist tech is not just a passing trend but a movement towards simplicity, sustainability, mindfulness, and ethics in technology. As technology continues to evolve, these emerging trends will shape the future of technology and guide us towards a more mindful and responsible digital age.

The impact of minimalist tech on society and the environment

The rise of minimalist tech has the potential to bring about significant positive impacts on both society and the environment. As people become more mindful of their technology consumption habits and shift towards minimalism, they can reduce the negative effects of excessive technology use and promote sustainability.

One of the most significant ways that minimalist tech can impact society is by improving well-being. By adopting minimalist tech practices, people can reduce the amount of time they spend on technology and instead focus on other activities that promote physical, mental, and emotional health. For example, people might spend more time engaging in physical activity, spending time with loved ones, or pursuing hobbies that bring them joy. By prioritizing these activities, people can improve their overall quality of life and reduce the negative effects of technology addiction, such as anxiety, depression, and social isolation.

In addition to improving well-being, minimalist tech can also help promote sustainability and reduce the negative environmental impacts of technology. One of the primary ways this is accomplished is through the reduction of e-waste. As people shift towards minimalism, they tend to consume fewer electronics and dispose of them less frequently. This can help reduce the amount of electronic waste that ends up in landfills, where it can take hundreds of years to decompose and release harmful toxins into the environment.

Another way that minimalist tech can promote sustainability is through energy conservation. Many electronics consume significant amounts of energy, and the production and distribution of that energy can have significant negative environmental impacts. By consuming fewer electronics and adopting energy-saving practices, people can reduce their overall energy consumption and promote sustainability.

Finally, minimalist tech can also promote social and environmental justice. Many of the materials and resources required to produce electronics are sourced from developing countries, where labor and environmental regulations may be lax or nonexistent. This can result in the exploitation of workers and significant environmental degradation. By reducing demand for electronics and promoting sustainable practices, people can help reduce these negative impacts and promote more just and equitable systems of production and consumption.

In conclusion, minimalist tech has the potential to bring about significant positive impacts on both society and the environment. By reducing excessive technology consumption, people can improve well-being, promote sustainability, and support more just and equitable systems of production and consumption. As the trend towards minimalist tech continues to grow, we can expect to see more significant positive impacts on society and the environment in the years to come.

The potential benefits and drawbacks of minimalist tech

As technology continues to advance, the minimalist approach to tech is becoming increasingly popular. While this approach offers numerous benefits, it also presents certain drawbacks. In this section, we'll explore both the potential benefits and drawbacks of minimalist tech.

Potential Benefits of Minimalist Tech:

1. Increased Productivity: One of the biggest benefits of minimalist tech is increased productivity. By minimizing distractions, simplifying tasks, and prioritizing focus, people can get more done in less time. This approach can lead to a greater sense of accomplishment, satisfaction, and even happiness.

2. Reduced Stress: Another benefit of minimalist tech is that it can help reduce stress levels. By minimizing the number of apps, emails, and notifications that compete for our attention, people can create a calmer, more peaceful environment. This can lead to lower stress levels, improved mental health, and better overall well-being.

3. Improved Health: By reducing the amount of time spent using tech devices, minimalist tech can also lead to improved

physical health. Research has shown that prolonged use of technology can lead to poor posture, eye strain, and other physical health problems. By practicing mindful consumption and minimalism in tech, people can reduce their risk of these health issues.

4. Environmental Benefits: By using technology less and adopting a minimalist approach to tech, individuals can also contribute to environmental sustainability. Fewer devices and less consumption can lead to less e-waste, which is a major contributor to environmental pollution.

5. Financial Savings: Adopting a minimalist tech approach can also lead to financial savings. By buying fewer devices and using them for longer, individuals can save money on the cost of purchasing new devices, as well as on energy costs associated with their use.

Potential Drawbacks of Minimalist Tech:

1. Limited Functionality: One of the main drawbacks of minimalist tech is that it may not offer the same functionality as more advanced devices. For example, a minimalist phone may not have all the features and capabilities of a smartphone. This limitation can be challenging for people who rely on certain features and apps for their work or personal life.

2. Social Isolation: Another potential drawback of minimalist tech is that it can lead to social isolation. By using technology less and reducing digital consumption, people may miss out on important social interactions and opportunities. Additionally, minimalism can lead to a lack of diversity in the media and information people consume, which can be detrimental to personal growth and understanding.

3. Learning Curve: Adopting a minimalist approach to tech can also require a significant learning curve. People may need to adjust to new devices or platforms, which can be challenging and time-consuming.

4. Compatibility Issues: Another potential issue with minimalist tech is that it may not be compatible with certain software or hardware. This can be particularly problematic for people who rely on specific tools or programs for their work.

5. Job Disruption: Finally, minimalist tech can also potentially disrupt certain industries and job markets. For example, the rise of automation and AI may lead to job loss in certain sectors, while the decline of traditional media may lead to fewer job opportunities in journalism and other related fields.

Conclusion:

As we can see, the minimalist approach to tech has both potential benefits and drawbacks. By prioritizing productivity, reducing stress, improving health, and contributing to environmental sustainability, minimalist tech can offer many advantages. However, it can also lead to limited functionality, social isolation, a steep learning curve, compatibility issues, and potential job disruption. As technology continues to evolve, it's important to carefully consider the impact of minimalist tech and make informed decisions about its adoption.

Predictions for the future of minimalist tech

The minimalist approach to technology has gained momentum in recent years, and many experts predict that it will continue to grow in popularity. Here are some predictions for the future of minimalist tech:

1. Increased Focus on Sustainability: With climate change becoming a more pressing issue, there will be a greater emphasis on sustainability in technology. Minimalist tech will play a significant role in reducing e-waste and encouraging more responsible consumption of electronics.

2. Growth of Minimalist Product Lines: As more consumers embrace minimalist tech, there will likely be an increase in the number of minimalist product lines. Companies may

develop simpler, more streamlined devices that are designed with minimalism in mind, as well as products that are specifically marketed to the minimalist community.

3. Continued Rise of the Digital Minimalism Movement: The digital minimalism movement is already gaining traction, and it is likely to continue to grow in popularity. More people are becoming aware of the negative effects of digital overload and are seeking ways to reduce their dependence on technology.

4. Increasing Emphasis on Privacy: As technology continues to become more integrated into our daily lives, privacy concerns will become more prevalent. Minimalist tech may offer a solution to these concerns by providing simpler, more transparent products that are designed to protect user privacy.

5. Greater Demand for Tech-Free Spaces: As people become more aware of the negative effects of technology on mental health, there will likely be a greater demand for tech-free spaces. These spaces may be dedicated to mindfulness, relaxation, or simply unplugging from technology for a period of time.

6. New Technologies that Support Minimalism: As minimalist tech continues to gain popularity, there will likely be new technologies that emerge to support this movement.

For example, we may see new software and apps that help people reduce their digital clutter or make it easier to use technology in a more mindful way.

7. Increased Collaboration between Minimalist and Sustainable Tech Movements: The minimalist and sustainable tech movements share many of the same goals, and we may see more collaboration between these two communities in the future. Together, they can work to create a more responsible and sustainable approach to technology.

Overall, the future of minimalist tech looks bright. As more people become aware of the benefits of a simpler, more mindful approach to technology, we can expect to see a continued shift toward minimalist tech products and practices. By prioritizing sustainability, privacy, and mindfulness, we can create a more responsible and balanced relationship with technology.

Chapter 8: Minimalism in Action: Case Studies

Case studies of companies and individuals who practice minimalist tech

In this chapter, we will examine case studies of companies and individuals who have successfully implemented minimalist tech practices into their daily routines. By studying these examples, we can gain insights into how minimalist tech can be applied in various contexts, and how it can lead to more productive and fulfilling lives.

1. Apple

Apple is known for its sleek and minimalist design aesthetic, and this approach extends to its technology as well. Apple's products are designed to be user-friendly and intuitive, with a focus on simplicity and functionality. The company has also implemented a number of eco-friendly practices, such as using recycled materials in its products and minimizing packaging waste.

2. Google

Google has a reputation for being a leader in innovative technology, but the company also places a high value on minimalist design. Its products, such as the Google search engine and the Chrome browser, are designed to be easy to use and visually appealing. Google has also implemented a number of initiatives to reduce its environmental impact, such as using renewable energy sources and reducing water usage.

3. Marie Kondo

Marie Kondo is a Japanese organizing consultant and author who has gained worldwide fame for her minimalist approach to home organization. Her philosophy, known as the KonMari method, encourages people to declutter their homes and keep only the possessions that bring them joy. Kondo's methods have been adapted by many people and have inspired a broader movement towards minimalism in various aspects of life.

4. Leo Babauta

Leo Babauta is the creator of Zen Habits, a popular blog focused on mindfulness and minimalism. Babauta's writing emphasizes the importance of simplifying one's life and reducing distractions in order to achieve greater focus and clarity. He also emphasizes the importance of sustainability and reducing one's environmental impact.

5. Joshua Fields Millburn and Ryan Nicodemus

Joshua Fields Millburn and Ryan Nicodemus are the creators of The Minimalists, a blog and podcast focused on minimalist living. The duo promotes the idea that living with less can lead to greater happiness and fulfillment, and they offer practical tips for simplifying one's life. They also place a strong emphasis on the environmental benefits of minimalist living.

6. Colin Wright

Colin Wright is a writer and minimalist who has gained a large following through his blog, books, and speaking engagements. Wright's philosophy emphasizes the importance of intentional living and the pursuit of experiences over possessions. He has also written extensively on the environmental benefits of minimalism and sustainable living.

7. Tiny Houses

The tiny house movement is a growing trend in minimalist living that involves living in smaller, more efficient homes. These homes are often designed to be eco-friendly, with features such as solar panels, composting toilets, and rainwater collection systems. The movement has gained popularity in recent years as a way to reduce environmental impact and simplify one's life.

In conclusion, these case studies demonstrate the diverse ways in which minimalist tech can be applied in various contexts. From tech giants like Apple and Google to individual bloggers and lifestyle experts, minimalist tech has proven to be a powerful tool for achieving greater focus, clarity, and sustainability. By studying these examples, we can gain valuable insights into how to incorporate minimalist tech practices into our own lives, and how to work towards a more mindful and fulfilling future.

The benefits and challenges of minimalist tech in action

Minimalist tech is gaining momentum as a way to reduce stress, increase productivity, and decrease the environmental impact of technology. As we've seen in previous chapters, minimalist tech is about being intentional with our use of technology and focusing on what truly matters.

In this chapter, we will explore case studies of companies and individuals who practice minimalist tech and the benefits and challenges they have encountered.

Benefits of Minimalist Tech in Action

1. Increased Productivity: Companies that have adopted minimalist tech practices have seen an increase in productivity. By eliminating distractions and focusing on essential tasks, employees can complete work efficiently.

2. Reduced Stress: Individuals who practice minimalist tech report feeling less overwhelmed and stressed. By reducing screen time and notifications, they can focus on other activities and live in the present moment.

3. Enhanced Creativity: Minimalist tech can also promote creativity. By stepping away from screens and technology, individuals can stimulate their minds and generate new ideas.

4. Improved Mental Health: Mindful use of technology can have a positive impact on mental health. By reducing exposure to negative content, individuals can avoid feelings of anxiety and depression.

Challenges of Minimalist Tech in Action

1. Resistance to Change: Adopting minimalist tech practices can be challenging for individuals and companies who are used to traditional tech practices. It requires a shift in mindset and habits, which can be difficult.

2. Fear of Missing Out (FOMO): Individuals may fear missing out on important information or social events if they limit their use of technology. This fear can make it challenging to adopt minimalist tech practices.

3. Increased Responsibility: Minimalist tech practices require individuals to take more responsibility for their use of technology. Without relying on notifications and constant connectivity, individuals must be more proactive in managing their time and tasks.

4. Limited Access: In some cases, minimalist tech practices may limit access to certain resources or information. For example, reducing screen time may limit access to news and information sources.

Case Studies of Minimalist Tech in Action

1. Basecamp: Basecamp is a software company that creates collaboration tools for remote teams. They have a strict no-meeting policy and prioritize asynchronous communication to reduce distractions and interruptions.

2. Digital Minimalism by Cal Newport: Cal Newport is a computer science professor and author of "Digital

Minimalism," which advocates for mindful use of technology. He practices minimalist tech by limiting his use of social media and using a flip phone instead of a smartphone.

3. A Life Less Throwaway by Tara Button: Tara Button is the founder of BuyMeOnce, a company that promotes sustainable consumerism. She practices minimalist tech by limiting her use of technology and promoting products that are durable and long-lasting.

4. The Slow Home Podcast: The Slow Home Podcast is a podcast that promotes intentional living and minimalism. Hosts Brooke McAlary and Ben McAlary encourage listeners to reduce their dependence on technology and focus on what truly matters.

Conclusion

The benefits of minimalist tech in action are clear: increased productivity, reduced stress, enhanced creativity, and improved mental health. However, challenges such as resistance to change and fear of missing out must be overcome to fully realize these benefits.

Case studies of companies and individuals who practice minimalist tech provide real-world examples of how these practices can be implemented successfully. By taking responsibility for our use of technology and being intentional with our choices, we can achieve a more mindful and fulfilling relationship with technology.

Lessons learned from successful minimalist tech implementations

Minimalism is not just a philosophy; it is a way of life that can be applied to everything, including technology. As the world becomes more technologically advanced, it's important to consider how we can use it in a more minimalist way. In this chapter, we will look at some successful case studies of minimalist tech implementations and the lessons we can learn from them.

Case Study 1: Apple

Apple is a company that is known for its minimalist design. From its sleek and simple hardware designs to its clean and easy-to-use software interfaces, Apple has always placed a high value on minimalism. Apple's minimalist approach has resulted in a loyal customer base that appreciates the company's focus on simplicity and ease of use.

One of the key lessons we can learn from Apple is the importance of focusing on the user experience. By keeping things simple and easy to use, Apple has created products that appeal to a broad range of users, regardless of their level of technical expertise. This is an important lesson for any company or individual looking to implement minimalist tech.

Case Study 2: Google

Google is another company that has embraced minimalism in its design and user interfaces. The company's search engine, for example, is a model of minimalist design, with a clean and uncluttered interface that focuses solely on delivering relevant search results.

Google's minimalist approach has also been applied to its hardware products, such as the Chromebook, which is a simple and affordable laptop that is designed for basic computing needs. The Chromebook is a great example of how minimalist tech can be used to create affordable and accessible products for a broad range of users.

One of the key lessons we can learn from Google is the importance of simplicity in design. By keeping things simple and focusing on the essentials, Google has created products that are easy to use and accessible to a wide range of users.

Case Study 3: Leo Babauta

Leo Babauta is a blogger and author who has embraced minimalist tech in his personal and professional life. Babauta is the founder of the popular blog Zen Habits, which focuses on simplicity, minimalism, and mindfulness. He is also the author of several books on minimalism and productivity.

Babauta's approach to minimalist tech is centered around the idea of simplifying his digital life. This includes using simple tools and software, minimizing distractions, and focusing on the essentials. Babauta has found that by simplifying his tech, he is able to be more productive and focused on the things that matter most to him.

One of the key lessons we can learn from Babauta is the importance of being intentional about our use of technology. By being mindful of how we use technology, we can make better choices about which tools and platforms we use, and how we use them. This can help us to be more productive, less stressed, and more fulfilled in our daily lives.

Conclusion

These case studies provide valuable insights into the benefits of minimalist tech and the lessons we can learn from successful implementations. Whether you are an individual looking to simplify your digital life or a company looking to create minimalist tech products, these case studies demonstrate that simplicity and focus are key to success.

By focusing on the user experience, simplicity in design, and being intentional about our use of technology, we can create minimalist tech products and practices that are accessible, affordable, and easy to use. As technology continues to evolve, it is important that we embrace minimalism as a way to create products and practices that are both ethical and sustainable.

The potential for scale and impact with minimalist tech
The rise of minimalist tech has shown us that less is often more when it comes to technology. In this chapter, we explore the potential for scale and impact with minimalist tech, particularly when it comes to creating solutions for the world's most pressing problems.

Minimalist tech can help address a range of issues, from environmental sustainability to social justice to healthcare. By focusing on simplicity, efficiency, and user-centered design, minimalist tech can create solutions that are more accessible, affordable, and effective than traditional technology.

One example of the potential for minimalist tech to create impact is in the field of healthcare. Traditional medical devices and equipment can be expensive, complex, and difficult to use, particularly in low-resource settings. Minimalist tech solutions, such as low-cost diagnostic tools and mobile health apps, can help address these challenges and improve access to healthcare for underserved populations.

Another area where minimalist tech can have a significant impact is in environmental sustainability. The world is facing urgent environmental challenges, from climate change to resource depletion to pollution. Minimalist tech solutions, such as energy-efficient devices, sustainable materials, and circular economy models, can help address these challenges and create a more sustainable future.

In addition to healthcare and environmental sustainability, minimalist tech can also play a role in social justice. Technology has the power to connect people, amplify voices, and facilitate social change. Minimalist tech solutions, such as community-driven platforms, digital storytelling tools, and open-source software, can help empower communities and facilitate social movements.

However, while the potential for impact with minimalist tech is significant, there are also challenges to overcome. One challenge is the need to balance simplicity with functionality. Minimalist tech solutions should be simple and easy to use, but they also need to be effective and meet the needs of their users. Achieving this balance requires a deep understanding of user needs and a commitment to user-centered design.

Another challenge is the need to scale and sustain minimalist tech solutions. Creating effective solutions is just the first step; to create real impact, these solutions need to be scaled and adopted widely. This requires strong partnerships, funding, and support, as well as a commitment to ongoing evaluation and improvement.

Despite these challenges, the potential for scale and impact with minimalist tech is significant. By focusing on simplicity, efficiency, and user-centered design, minimalist tech solutions can create meaningful change in a range of fields. The key is to remain committed to these principles and to work collaboratively to create solutions that are accessible, affordable, and effective for all.

Conclusion

The potential for technology and minimalism to create a more sustainable and fulfilling future

The world we live in today is constantly evolving, and technology is at the forefront of that evolution. With advancements in technology, we have been able to accomplish things we never thought possible. However, with great power comes great responsibility. The negative impact of technology on the environment and our lives has become more apparent, and it is clear that something must be done.

Minimalism is a movement that has gained traction in recent years, as people seek to simplify their lives and reduce their impact on the environment. The principles of minimalism can be applied to technology, and this has led to the emergence of minimalist tech. This new approach to technology is focused on creating products and services that are simple, efficient, and sustainable.

In this book, we have explored the benefits and challenges of minimalist tech, as well as strategies for reducing digital consumption and ethical considerations in technology. We have also looked at case studies of companies and individuals who have successfully implemented minimalist tech, and the lessons we can learn from them.

As we conclude this book, it is clear that the potential for technology and minimalism to create a more sustainable and fulfilling future is immense. By adopting minimalist tech, we can reduce our impact on the environment, increase our productivity, and live more fulfilling lives. We can also ensure that technology is used in a responsible and ethical way, with the interests of society and the environment at its core.

The potential for scale and impact with minimalist tech is enormous. With the right approach and mindset, we can transform the way we interact with technology and create a better future for ourselves and future generations. We must work together to create a more sustainable and fulfilling future, and minimalist tech can help us achieve this goal.

In conclusion, this book has been an exploration of the possibilities and potential of minimalist tech. We hope that it has inspired you to think differently about technology and its role in your life, and that you will join us on this journey towards a more sustainable and fulfilling future.

The challenges and opportunities of adopting a minimalist tech approach

As we wrap up our exploration of minimalist tech, it's important to consider both the challenges and opportunities that come with adopting this approach. While minimalist tech has the potential to create a more sustainable and fulfilling future, there are also significant obstacles to overcome.

One of the main challenges of minimalist tech is the entrenched cultural norms and economic incentives that drive the technology industry. As we've seen throughout this book, the prevailing business model for tech companies is to maximize user engagement and monetize data. This means that many of the devices, apps, and platforms we use are designed to be addictive and time-consuming, rather than efficient and purposeful.

To shift towards minimalist tech, we'll need to find ways to incentivize companies to prioritize sustainability, ethical practices, and user well-being. This may require regulatory changes, as well as changes in consumer behavior. For example, if we start valuing products that are durable, repairable, and designed to last, rather than disposable and replaceable, companies will have more of an incentive to invest in sustainable practices.

Another challenge of minimalist tech is that it requires a certain level of privilege and access. Not everyone has the luxury of being able to disconnect from technology or choose to use more expensive, but sustainable products. In order to create a truly equitable and sustainable future, we'll need to address issues of economic inequality and ensure that everyone has access to the resources they need to make informed choices about their tech use.

Despite these challenges, there are many opportunities that come with adopting a minimalist tech approach. For one, minimalist tech can help us live more intentionally and deliberately. By reducing our digital distractions and focusing on the tools and devices that truly serve our needs, we can create more space for the things that matter most, whether that's building meaningful relationships, pursuing creative hobbies, or simply enjoying the present moment.

Minimalist tech can also help us reduce our carbon footprint and mitigate the negative impacts of technology on the environment. By choosing products that are designed to last, we can reduce the amount of waste we produce and conserve resources. By being more intentional about our tech use, we can also reduce our energy consumption and carbon emissions.

Finally, adopting a minimalist tech approach can help us foster more ethical and sustainable values in our society. As we've seen throughout this book, technology has the power to shape our beliefs, behaviors, and norms in powerful ways. By consciously choosing to use technology in ways that align with our values, we can help create a more just and sustainable future for everyone.

In conclusion, minimalist tech is not a one-size-fits-all solution, and there are certainly challenges to overcome. However, by being intentional and deliberate about our tech use, we can create a more sustainable and fulfilling future for ourselves and our communities. Whether we're individual consumers, tech companies, or policymakers, we all have a role to play in shaping the future of technology in ways that serve the greater good.

The call to action for individuals and organizations to embrace mindful tech practices

As we conclude our exploration of minimalist tech, it is clear that there is a pressing need for individuals and organizations to embrace mindful tech practices. We have seen the potential benefits of minimalism, including increased productivity, reduced environmental impact, and improved well-being. However, there are also significant challenges to implementing a minimalist tech approach, including the need for behavior change, the pressure to keep up with technological advancements, and the difficulty of balancing sustainability with profitability.

Despite these challenges, the potential rewards of adopting a minimalist tech approach are too great to ignore. The growing concern about the environmental impact of technology, the negative effects on mental health, and the need for more sustainable business practices all point towards the necessity of embracing mindful tech practices.

For individuals, adopting a minimalist tech approach means being more intentional about our technology use. We can start by examining our own habits and identifying areas where we can reduce our digital consumption. We can also prioritize ethical tech practices, such as choosing products from companies that prioritize sustainability and privacy, and advocating for policies that protect consumer rights.

For organizations, embracing minimalist tech practices can lead to improved productivity and sustainability, while also enhancing brand reputation and customer loyalty. Companies can start by implementing policies that prioritize sustainable tech practices, such as reducing e-waste and promoting energy-efficient technologies. Additionally, companies can adopt ethical tech practices that prioritize user privacy and data protection.

In conclusion, the call to action for individuals and organizations is clear. It is time to embrace mindful tech practices and take steps towards a more sustainable and fulfilling future. By working together to prioritize ethical and sustainable tech practices, we can create a world where technology serves us, rather than the other way around. It is up to all of us to make a difference and shape the future of technology in a positive way.

THE END

To help you better understand the language and concepts related to aging and older adults, below you will find a list of key terms and their definitions.

Key terms and definitions

1. Minimalism: A lifestyle that focuses on living with less and simplifying one's possessions and surroundings.

2. Mindful consumption: Being conscious of the impact of one's purchasing and consumption habits on oneself, others, and the environment.

3. Sustainable: Capable of being maintained or continued over a long period of time without depleting natural resources or causing harm to the environment.

4. Digital detox: A period of time during which a person refrains from using digital devices, particularly smartphones and social media, in order to reduce stress and improve mental health.

5. Ethical tech: The development and use of technology that is aligned with ethical principles and values, such as fairness, privacy, and transparency.

6. Digital well-being: The ability to maintain a healthy balance between technology use and other aspects of life, such as social interactions, physical exercise, and mental health.

7. Screen time: The amount of time a person spends using digital devices, such as smartphones, tablets, and computers, to access the internet or engage in other activities.

8. E-waste: Electronic waste, which refers to discarded electronic devices and components, such as computers, smartphones, and batteries, that pose environmental and health hazards when not disposed of properly.

9. Attention economy: The economic system that relies on the attention of consumers as a scarce resource that can be monetized by digital platforms and advertisers.

10. User experience (UX): The overall experience that a person has when interacting with a digital product or service, including ease of use, accessibility, and enjoyment.

Supporting Materials

Introduction:

Kim, K. (2017). Goodbye, Things: The New Japanese Minimalism. Hachette UK.

Millburn, J. F., & Nicodemus, R. (2010). Minimalism: Live a Meaningful Life. Asymmetrical Press.

Chapter 1: The History of Technology and Minimalism:

Klinenberg, E. (2018). Palaces for the People: How Social Infrastructure Can Help Fight Inequality, Polarization, and the Decline of Civic Life. Broadway Books.

Glei, J. (2016). Unsubscribe: How to Kill Email Anxiety, Avoid Distractions, and Get Real Work Done. PublicAffairs.

Chapter 2: The Basics of Blockchain:

Tapscott, D., & Tapscott, A. (2018). Blockchain revolution: how the technology behind bitcoin and other cryptocurrencies is changing the world. Penguin.

Chapter 3: The Basics of AI:

Domingos, P. (2015). The master algorithm: How the quest for the ultimate learning machine will remake our world. Basic Books.

Chapter 4: The Minimalist Approach to Tech:

Newport, C. (2016). Deep Work: Rules for Focused Success in a Distracted World. Grand Central Publishing.

Harris, T. (2016). The Minimalist Mindset: The Practical
Path to Making Your Passions a Priority and to Retaking
Your Freedom. Createspace Independent Publishing
Platform.

Chapter 5: Mindful Consumption in the Digital Age:

Sinek, S. (2019). The Infinite Game. Portfolio/Penguin.

Lerner, M. J. (2019). The Art of Productivity: Your
Competitive Edge. Martin Lerner.

Chapter 6: The Ethics of Technology:

Turkle, S. (2017). Alone together: Why we expect more from
technology and less from each other. Basic Books.

Winner, L. (1986). The whale and the reactor: A search for
limits in an age of high technology. University of Chicago
Press.

Chapter 7: The Future of Minimalist Tech:

Lowenstein, R. (2019). The End of Tech Companies.
Penguin.

Bilton, N. (2017). American Kingpin: The Epic Hunt for the
Criminal Mastermind Behind the Silk Road. Penguin.

Chapter 8: Minimalism in Action: Case Studies:

Sharma, R. (2018). The 5 AM Club: Own Your Morning,
Elevate Your Life. HarperCollins.

Sivers, D. (2011). Anything You Want: 40 Lessons for a New
Kind of Entrepreneur. The Domino Project.

Conclusion:

Iyengar, S. S. (2010). The Art of Choosing. Twelve.

Csikszentmihalyi, M. (2008). Flow: The psychology of optimal experience. Harper & Row.